THE GOD WHO CHANGES LIVES

Volume Two

The God Who Changes Lives

Volume Two

Edited by Mark Elsdon-Dew

Cook Ministry Resources
Colorado Springs, Colorado/Paris, Ontario

Front cover and text illustrations by Charlie Mackesy.

Editor's Acknowledgements

This book could never have been published without the support and kindness of all the contributors, who not only allowed me to interview them at length about their personal lives, but have checked and re-checked the text. I am enormously grateful to each of them.
I would like to thank Tanya Ivas, who conducted two of the interviews, and also Linda Williams and Louise Allen for all their help throughout the process of producing a final manuscript.

Contents

"Write down for the coming generation what the Lord has done, so that people not yet born will praise him."

Psalm 102:18

Alpha

Many of the contributors to this book make reference to the Alpha course, a practical introduction to the Christian faith that has had a remarkable impact on many people's lives. This 10-week course first started at Holy Trinity Brompton Church in London. Alpha has proved so popular that it is now running in tens of thousands of churches across Britain, North America, and the world.

Foreword

by Sandy Millar
Vicar of Holy Trinity Brompton

It gives me enormous pleasure to write the Foreword for Volume Two of *The God Who Changes Lives*. It often surprises me that bad news receives so much attention from those who report the "news" locally or nationally whereas good news, news about what God is doing, scarcely gets a mention. Well, here is another volume of good news.

Volume One has sold more than 40,000 copies in the world already and I have no doubt this will too; most people at least are thrilled to hear about God's kindness and power. They long to believe that He is still at work today.

Most of the people whose stories are told in this book are known personally to me; "ordinary" people with very little, if anything, in common but the fact that God has touched their lives in some real way—the God who literally changes lives.

This is their story and I feel sure that, as you read it, you will be as moved, encouraged and challenged as I have been once again by the simplicity, the love and the power of God.

"Sing praise to the LORD; tell the wonderful things he has done."
Psalm 105:2

Introduction

by Mark Elsdon-Dew

As a journalist who enjoys a "good story," I love to hear people describe how their lives have been changed by God.

Again and again I hear people speak about how an encounter with God has completely turned their lives around. This has resulted in restored relationships, changed lifestyles, tragedy faced with fortitude, or simply new purpose and direction.

So when I brought a collection of these stories together under the title *The God Who Changes Lives* in 1995, I was glad to find that others found them as fascinating as I did. Indeed the response has been so encouraging that now, some two and a half years later, I have been encouraged to produce a second volume.

Once again the stories in this book are almost all the results of interviews conducted with members of the congregation of Holy Trinity Brompton or those associated in some way with the church.

I would like to pay tribute to all those who have agreed to open up their lives in this way. It is often difficult for us, the readers, to appreciate how vulnerable the individuals concerned feel in doing this, but I know they have chosen to do so in order that others may appreciate that Jesus Christ is alive today.

Although these stories are mostly linked to Holy Trinity Brompton, there is nothing special about our church. It is the unique God we worship who is special—and He can be encountered in tens of thousands of other churches all over the country and the world.

And the purpose of this book?

As John wrote at the end of his Gospel, "These have been written in order that you may believe that Jesus is the Messiah, the Son of God, and that through your faith in him you may have life."

I do hope you will be inspired as you read it.

"Whoever looks for me can find me."
Proverbs 8:17

1

"Every time I saw my son, Clinton, it would be great, but then when I left he would break down and cry."

The story of Paul Cowley

As a young man, Paul Cowley ended up in prison and later, after a brief marriage, became estranged from his son, Clinton. Here, Paul tells the remarkable story of how God changed his life and how, following prayer, he was reconciled with the son whom he had not seen for more than six years.

I left home when I was 15 because I was bit of a rebel and my mom and dad couldn't really handle it. Soon after, my father divorced my mother. When I asked him why he had divorced, he said he had only married because I was there and when I left home there was nothing left of their relationship. So they split up. For the next five years I had a variety of jobs. I was a butcher, I was a milkman, I worked in a bakery—different things like that. I lived in various apartments and got involved with some skinheads—a real punk rock crowd—who were the rage at the time. For five years I just rode around in that scene. I was doing everything that you shouldn't do. I was into a lot of things and building up a life of crime. I got myself a criminal record for petty stuff—basically stealing cars and joyriding.

When I was 20 I started to realize that my life was going downhill and that I needed to do something. At that time, I saw a billboard seeking recruits for something called "Adventurous Training" and I decided to sign up. It was a bit touch-and-go because of my criminal record, but they selected me and I went into the Artillery, undergoing basic training at Woolwich in London. I enlisted for three years and seemed to fit in right away. The things I got into trouble for on the street, the Army promoted me for! It was stable and people gave me responsibility.

> **! The things I got into trouble for on the street, the Army promoted me for!**

Around that time, I met Lynn who became my girlfriend. After my training, I was assigned to Germany and we had to make a decision either to get married or separate because she couldn't go with me as a girlfriend. She had to be a wife. So we got married.

A year later, we had a little boy—Clinton. We were living in Hohna in Germany, on the northwest side near the border with Russia and I was throwing myself into my work. I went into everything and was hungry for promotion. I didn't care who I stepped on or what I did. The only thing I wanted was to get out of being a non-ranker to getting some rank—which I did quite quickly. I made Staff Sergeant in four and a half years—which is quite unknown in the Artillery. It usually takes about eight or nine years. I was quite ruthless to get there. During that time, my relationship with Lynn started to deteriorate. We didn't get along very well. I took another assignment—to get promoted—back at Chester in England.

While we were in Chester we ended up getting divorced because it just wasn't working. It was mostly my fault because I had become a workaholic. I didn't value my relationship with my wife. I was more interested in other things. Clinton was three then. It didn't really bother me leaving Clinton at the time. I didn't take Lynn seriously or my commitment to having a child seriously. Life was about *me*. Lynn and Clinton were a bit incidental. They were slowing my promotion prospects down.

I pursued my career in the Army in single housing. The Adventurous Training took me all over the place—Canada, Germany, Gibraltar. I was an instructor in mountain climbing, skiing, canoeing, and white-water rafting, and would take expeditions all over the place. I was looking for promotions and adventure all the time.

At this time, I saw Clinton off and on whenever I could fit him in. The years went by. Occasionally, I would arrange for Clinton to fly out to where I was so that we could have a week or weekend together. I had a variety of different relationships with women in those days, so he would come out and meet them.

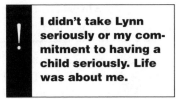

I didn't take Lynn seriously or my commitment to having a child seriously. Life was about me.

If I was back in England we would sometimes have a few days together between my flights, but it wasn't a priority. I also visited my mother and father when I was in the country, but I didn't tell my father that I had seen my mother, because he would get really angry. When I saw my mom I didn't mention my dad either.

In between I tried to see Clinton as well. Every time I saw him it would be great, but when I left he would break down and cry. He wanted to be with me but I couldn't cope with that. All this drove me crazy. I couldn't deal with the emotional or physical stress. I was lying to my father about my mother and to my mother about my father. So I decided to escape, as I always did. I took a job in Cyprus teaching climbing. They wanted someone to go out there for two or three weeks but I extended it to ten weeks and then just stayed out there.

One day I was teaching junior soldiers to climb in a big ravine when we heard voices at the bottom. My climbing partner said, "There are girls down there." And I said, "I don't think so. Not around here. Only sheep and trees!"

We climbed down a bit further and at the bottom were two girls sitting on a rock, doing some painting. We got to talking and found out that they were named Amanda and Kristina and that they were art students traveling around the island drawing the countryside. They were on an exchange for six or seven weeks with an art college in Cyprus. I invited them back to the camp. I wanted to be friends with both of them, but I ended up falling in love with Amanda.

When I got back to England I went to see her in London. We were both quite marriage-phobic, because of the breakdown in relationships in both our families. Her parents were divorced too, so the idea of marriage wasn't even a consideration. We just lived together in what we called a long "engagement" that lasted eight years.

During that time, my mother became ill with cancer. I was stationed in Warwickshire at the time and Amanda and I had a house there, so my mother came and lived in our house. Not long afterward she died. It was quite a blow really because I was just getting a relationship back with her. I was really angry, but Amanda was amazing. She guided me and took control. It was a really difficult time.

While we were sorting through my mom's stuff, I found a Bible— the *Good News Bible*. I looked inside it and there were lots of passages marked. There was also a name and telephone number. We called the number and spoke to a lady who turned out to be a friend of my mother's from Manchester.

I went to visit her and she told me that my mother had become a Christian about two years before she died. My mom had never said anything about it at all. She had kept it quite secret. She used to go to church and she was just getting into a fellowship group when she left to live with us. That blew my socks off really, because my mom was a hard northern woman and quite volatile. I couldn't fathom the idea of her being a Christian.

My dad didn't want to come to mom's funeral at first because they hadn't seen each other for a long time. They were very much in love with each other, but it was a sort of "Burton and Taylor"-type marriage—incredibly intense—and they were both very angry with each other. I said it would be very special if he would come up to the funeral, which he did. It was very difficult for him. He got lost trying to find the cemetery and he was late. We were just putting mom into the earth when he turned up. He was really stressed about that.

Then we went back home, across the road to the house and we tried to talk about things. I realize now that he couldn't take the emotion of mom being dead. He tried to talk to me about all the guilt he felt, but he just got upset. He got into his car and took off back to Manchester. After that, we had a falling out about some money and some possessions of my mom's that he wanted. My mom had left everything to me because I was the only relative she had. I took him around her house about a month later and said, "Dad, take what you want in the house. Whatever you want is yours. It is your furniture anyway." He got a bit angry about things and he was confused and mixed up. After that, I didn't see him for six years.

Occasionally Clinton would come and stay with us. He has always gotten along well with Amanda but gradually he stopped coming and we lost contact. I have to admit that Amanda was a far greater priority to me than he was at that time.

After 16 1/2 years in the Army, I was recruited for the position of fitness director of a men's health club in Mayfair. During that time Amanda really encouraged me to write to my father and to Clinton, which I found really difficult because I never got any replies back from either. She said, "You need to keep writing. You need to keep that channel open." So I would write. I would be a bit cynical about it, but I would keep writing. I never got any replies at all. When I felt melancholy, perhaps after looking at some photos of my mom, I would read her *Good News Bible.*

Soon after this, Amanda and I were visiting some friends in Rye on the south coast for the weekend. On a Sunday morning we went for a walk along the seafront and I suddenly said to her, "I want to go to church."

Amanda nearly fell over and said, "What do you mean you want to go to church?" I said, "Well, I just feel that I would like to go to church." She said, "You're probably going to be really bored." But we went—and I was really bored.

After that, for the next eight months, I went to every church you could possibly think of— with or without Amanda. I went to happy-clappy churches; I went to quiet churches; I went to Baptist, Methodist, Lutheran, Church of England, Catholic churches. I went to everything.

I went to churches that were filled with 700 people and I went to churches where there was me, two others, a vicar, and a cat. I would sit at the back and listen. I was compelled to do it. I got very bored, but I still kept going.

Then a work friend of Amanda's named Jessica suggested we try Holy Trinity Brompton. We walked into HTB one Sunday in 1992 and Tom Gillum [*now vicar of St. Stephen's, Westbourne Park*], was preaching. At the end of it he said, "If there is anyone here who is new to the church and would like to pray about whether this is the church for them, do come to the front and we'll get some ministry team to pray for you." So I said, "We might as well try this prayer stuff, Amanda. Let's have a go."

We went forward and found ourselves talking to Tom Gillum. He walked toward me and Amanda and we introduced ourselves. We told him what we were doing and how we were looking for a church.

He prayed a very simple prayer that I will never forget. He just put his hands on me and Amanda and he said, "Lord, I ask that You find these people a church. If it is this church then that will be fantastic, but if it isn't, Lord, I ask that You will plant them in an area where they will grow and develop their relationship with You."

I thought that was kind of a nice prayer. There was no pressure at all. He just said good-bye to us and hoped that he might see us again. I liked that, so I went back to the church. Then someone suggested the Alpha course and I thought, *If I was trying to be a mechanic I would go to maintenance classes.* This seemed to be a course for people who wanted to find out about God.

So I read the literature and we attended the course. We were put in a group with a man named Geoff Wilmot and I am sure I was Geoff Wilmot's nightmare. I must have asked every question. Amanda told me to be quiet on lots of occasions, but I knew nothing and I wanted to know everything. I wanted the whole 2,000 years of Christianity explained to me! He was great—so patient.

So Amanda and I did that course together. After that, we were asked to come back to help on the next course, so we did. Before the end of the second course, I stopped thinking about the "head" stuff and concentrated more on putting it in my heart. I remembered reading in the Bible where Jesus says, "You have to come to me as a child." I thought, *What does that mean: "a child"?* I thought about Clinton and how he would always trust me. So I thought, *I am going to come to him as a child* (Matthew 18). So I gave my life to Christ. I gave Him my heart and I committed myself to Him. Amanda, who had done something similar at the age of 13 but had never followed through on it, did the same a little bit later.

As soon as I allowed God to "get me," my whole concept of life completely changed. It was like the scales were removed. I had a different perspective on life completely. I started to reconsider my relationship with Amanda, because we weren't married. I began to think, *We should be married. What is this? We are sleeping together. We are living together. What is going on?* I just wasn't comfortable with it. So I went out and bought two old-fashioned engagement rings from an antique shop.

One day soon afterward, when Amanda and I were out shopping, we sat down in a coffee shop in West Hampstead and I pushed these two rings in a little box towards her. She opened them and said, "What do you want?"

"I think we should get engaged," I said.

She said, "I might not want to get engaged."

I said, "What do you mean you don't want to get engaged? I was going to ask you to marry me."

She said, "Well, I don't want to marry you."

So my whole world started to fall apart. I thought, *What is going on? What do you mean you don't want to marry me? You have got to marry me. We are Christians. We have got to do this stuff.*

After eight years of a great relationship, we went back to the apartment and broke up. We had an almighty fight and she left me. She went to stay with Kristina, the girl she had been to Cyprus with. I remember sitting that night in the apartment with a bottle of wine on my own thinking, *Great! This is a good plan Lord! I am now crying. I am on my own. I am drinking and what is going on? I am doing what you tell me to do. I have asked her to marry me and she has left me and we have had a big fight.*

Through that night I was in an agitated state and, although I didn't know it at the time, Amanda was too. I phoned her the next morning and I said, "Look, we need to talk."

We met at the Natural History Museum. We both took the day off from work and sat for five hours talking about stuff that we had to work out. In the end we got back together.

We were married in Leicestershire, in a little village called Sheepy Magna. The day after our wedding, we got baptized in a river behind the church. It was freezing. After our honeymoon, we got involved with running an Alpha group with Geraldine and Russell Garner. They have been an amazing influence on our lives, especially mine. After Alpha, we joined their home group, which was brilliant.

I started sharing stuff about my life and about Amanda's life. One night, after everyone had gone and it was just me and Amanda left, Geraldine said "Do you want to pray about anything? You are always praying for people and you never get prayed for yourself."

I said, "No, I'm fine. We don't need anything."

Geraldine said, "Well, what about your son and your father?"

I said, "No, they are fine. They are OK."

I realize now that there were two issues in my life at that time that I didn't want anyone to touch, because I had killed them off and they were gone—separate. She said, "Well, I think we should pray about it."

She prayed for a reconciliation with Clinton and a reconciliation with my father. I was very cynical and I said, "You're going to need a lot of help with that one!"

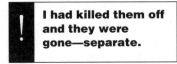

I had killed them off and they were gone—separate.

Every time we went there she would bring up, "Let's pray for Clinton," and the whole home group would end up praying for Clinton and my father. That just kept on, but my letters still weren't answered. I sent a letter to Clinton explaining what had happened, who Jesus was, what He had done to me, how He had changed me and my whole outlook on life was different. I sent the same sort of letter to my father. Still no replies.

What I didn't know was that Clinton was having a hard time. He had been expelled from school for drugs (which I didn't know about) and was heavily involved in the party scene.

His relationship with Lynn, his mother, and his stepfather, Phillip, was deteriorating. He was now 16 and Lynn just couldn't cope with his outbursts of anger, his not coming home, his staying out for days, and his drinking. In the end, she said, "I can't cope with you anymore, I want you out of this house." He went on to a party and after doing a "heavy session of drugs," he left and went for a walk. He ended up running in a field. He said he ran and ran and ran and then sat down under a tree and cried. He intended to kill himself. Then he cried out to God and said, "If there is anybody out there, then You had better come and help me." He slept in the field. The next morning he went home to his mom and she said, "I think you need to speak to your father because you are just like he was." That was how he came to call me.

So I got a phone call in my office out of the blue, "I want to come and see you, Dad."

"OK, when?"

"Today."

So I said, "When today?"

He said, "I'll be at King's Cross at seven o'clock."

I had not seen him or spoken to him for six years.

It was a Tuesday night—the night of our home group (by then we were running one of our own), so I told Amanda that I was going to need a lot of prayer cover for this. She got the whole group praying for this meeting at seven o'clock.

I turned up at King's Cross and saw him walking toward me. I had left a cute little boy but now this "thug" was walking toward me. He had dark glasses on and a small suitcase. It frightened the life out of me.

It was quite hard at first to talk. We went out that night for something to eat, just me and Clint. I took him home and he started to share our life there. We talked and we talked and we talked. We talked about Jesus.

> ! I had left a cute little boy but now this "thug" was walking toward me.

We talked about his life. We talked about the suicide attempt. We just talked about all sorts of things.

I managed to get him a job through a contact that I had, so he started work there. It put him in a suit, which meant he had to tidy himself up. I was praying a lot for Clinton to go to Alpha, but I didn't want to push it. In the end, one day as we were getting ready to go to a Sunday service, he said, "Oh, I'll come with you."

That was in January 1996. He came and he sat in church. Then he came again. He went from the hard aggressive stance, to the lighter stance, to standing up, to singing. Then he said, "I might do the Alpha course, Dad."

I said, "OK, that would be great." I was singing and dancing under my breath!

One night at home halfway through the course Clinton said, "I want you to talk to me a bit more about Jesus and all that stuff." So we did, Amanda and I. In the end we prayed together on the sofa and he gave his life to Christ then and there, which was amazing. Then his life started to change. He started to pray for things and he decided that his drugs are now out the window and he has stopped smoking.

Later that same week I got a phone call from my father saying that he wanted to see me. We had a strained phone call, but it was a start.

A little later, my father came to London to see us. We went and saw Clinton at his work and he and my father had quite a tearful reunion. He hadn't seen Clinton for over ten years. Then he even came to a service at Holy Trinity with us all and met our friends. After that, Clinton and I went to Macclesfield and spent a whole weekend with my dad—the first time we had all been together up there for 10 years. It is amazing to see how God has reunited me with my son and my dad. Only the power of Jesus could do such a thing.

Paul Cowley is now on the staff of Holy Trinity Brompton where he is responsible for the church's growing ministry in prisons. He and his wife Amanda have a daughter, born in February 1998.

"For the first time in my life I got on my hands and knees and said, 'God, if You are there, do something quick.' "

The story of Michaela Flanagan

Single mother Michaela Flanagan was in despair following the suicide of a close friend when she met up with a local Methodist minister and said, "I want to know about life." Here she describes what happened:

I was born in Chester, northwest England, and although my parents divorced when I was five, I had a happy childhood. Mom remarried and my stepfather and I have a good relationship. Apart from my grandparents, nobody in my family went to church.

I was good academically at school and we were taught religion, but I thought the Bible was just stories. At school, I wanted to be part of the "in crowd" who smoked, had boyfriends, went clubbing, and did all the rebellious things.

When I was 15, I became pregnant. It was a holiday romance with a lad from Italy but when I told him, he didn't want to know. I had a very immature view of motherhood. I thought it was about dressing up a baby in nice clothes and going for walks with a stroller. The reality was that I had to grow up instantly and I couldn't handle the responsibility.

After Daniel was born, Mom helped me at first but then I felt she was taking over so I left home and took my son with me. I went to stay with some people in Ellesmere Port, about 20 miles away. At 17, I had no job and I was surviving on Social Security payments. Four of us, including Daniel, were sleeping in a small room.

It was then I began to experiment with drugs. Eventually, Mom came and took Daniel away. She told me that if I didn't sort out my life, she would try and get custody of him. I was in a mess then, so I don't blame her. I moved into a shelter for the homeless and eventually the council got me a house in Helsby, a small town about 17 miles from Liverpool. Daniel was back with me, I had a little job and I was starting to get my life together. Then it all went terribly wrong.

I got involved with one of the main drug dealers in the area. This man was psychotic and he would terrorize me and make me feel worthless. Even though I was afraid of him, I lived with him for over a year. I tried everything to end the relationship but he would beat me up—although he was always very careful to hurt me where the bruises wouldn't show. He told me that it was my fault that he hit me. If I was prettier he wouldn't hit me. He hit me because I was ugly. By then, I was smoking a lot of marijuana and also taking LSD and speed. All my self-confidence vanished and I hated myself 100 percent.

Daniel had a very bad time. I would be beaten in front of him and the poor lad saw some horrible things. In the end, a friend found out what was happening and the police became involved. I had to go to court to get a restraining order to keep him away from me.

After that, I jumped into relationships. I just wanted some protection for me and Daniel. I was so scared of being on my own. I was getting more and more addicted to marijuana. I hated myself, I hated the mirror and I was devastated with how my life had turned out. There didn't seem to be a way out of it.

Then, about two and half years ago, Steven, who was a very close friend, killed himself. He'd split up with his girlfriend and had connected a pipe to his exhaust and pumped the fumes into his car. He was my age and nothing in my life had ever hit me that hard. I'd loved him, he was my friend and at the funeral I looked at his coffin and it struck me—where had he gone on to? It was really distressing.

I decided I would sort myself out and live my life to the full every day. My new positive attitude lasted about two weeks and I was back in the pit again. I thought that if Steven's death couldn't get me to shake myself up, then I must be a waste of space.

One day I was walking along the road and I saw Andrew Baguley [*Minister of Helsby Methodist Church*]. I'd seen him a few times because I used to hang around by the church with the gangs. I felt this amazing pull toward him and a sense that I had to ask him something. He seemed so lovely and I said to him, "I want to know about life because my friend has died and I'm in a mess. I want to know what's next and is this all there is for me?"

Andrew told me that a lot of the questions I had could be answered on the Alpha course that was going on at the church. "Would you like to come along?" he said.

I said, "Church? No chance. I don't think so!"

Then he simply said, "Well, I think you'd be really good at it, Michaela." Well, nobody has said anything like that to me for years, so I thought, *Oh! I might come then. I might be good at it!*

I went along to Alpha and I was so shocked. I thought Christians were really sad, boring people but I couldn't believe it—everyone was so happy. They all welcomed me and they were really nice to me. They wanted to talk to me, they were interested in me, they wanted to know about my life and what I'd done—that's what really struck me.

I listened to the first talk on "Who Was Jesus?" and I was enthralled. I'd never thought about Jesus before and when the worship started, tears were pouring from my eyes and I didn't know what was going on. Then we went into small groups and I felt sick with fear because everyone was talking and I wanted to go home.

I thought, *What am I doing here? I'm going mad, I've been on too many drugs*, and then I heard a voice in my head say to me, "Go and ask Peter about his life."

Peter was quite nice looking so I thought, *OK* and I went up to him and said, "I want to ask you why you are here," so he told me about his life. He told me about this guy called Jesus who he knew and to be honest, at the time I thought he was a bit of a nut case.

I went to the second talk (a talk titled "Why Did Jesus Die?") and the same thing happened again. During the worship I was in floods of tears and didn't know why. My friends were looking after Daniel and, by this time, they'd found out that I was going to church. They thought I'd gone soft in the head.

When I came home from the third talk, my friends were sitting around smoking marijuana. For the first time, I'd made up my mind to say no when they offered me some but in the end I did smoke it. I was really angry with myself and when they'd gone, I had a panic attack. I used to get them a lot. They were terrifying and my whole body would shake uncontrollably. As the attack went on, for the first time in my life I got on my hands and knees and said, "God, if You are there, do something quick!"

All of a sudden, this incredible peace filled the front room. Daniel's photograph was on the side and I felt my eyes drawn to his face. I heard a voice say, "Hold on tight Michaela. Look at Daniel's eyes—aren't his eyes, your eyes? Isn't he beautiful? Aren't you beautiful? Look at his face Michaela. He needs you." There was a glow around Daniel's face and he seemed to be coming out of the picture. That was it—the panic attack went completely.

After the third week of Alpha, I found out I was pregnant. I'd been living with a man off and on for about two years but he didn't want to have anything to do with the baby. It was the worst thing that could happen and I was devastated. The people from the church came round to my house and invited me to the Holy Spirit Day but I told them that I didn't want to do Alpha anymore.

I knew I couldn't cope with another baby on my own, so I went for an abortion. At the time, I didn't think about the church or about God—I had the abortion and just wanted to die. I thought I was the biggest piece of scum anyone had ever laid eyes on. I was utterly ridden with guilt and I lay on my bed for days not getting dressed but crying and crying, and wishing I had the strength to kill myself.

While I was in this mess, Andrew came to my house. I'd never been as low but that day I had a feeling that he would come. He said, "I know what's happened, Michaela. God told us." I thought, *God did! This guy knows nothing about me and he's come here telling me that God told him that I'd had an abortion. This is completely strange!*

Andrew said, "Don't be frightened. God loves you. Just ask Him for forgiveness and He'll straighten you out. He wants you to come to Him and know Him." I was crying my eyes out and felt completely broken. Andrew asked me to come back to Alpha and he prayed for me. I got dressed for the first time in days and went to the course. In the worship, I broke down sobbing.

It was the talk on healing and afterward, the ladies asked if they could pray for me. Something was starting to dawn in my head, so I agreed. They prayed and I felt a weight lifting off my head—I still wasn't convinced that there was a God, though.

A couple of days later, a lady came to speak at our church. She was David Watson's wife, Anne [*the late David Watson, a British evangelist who died in 1984*] and I was invited along. Wild horses wouldn't have kept me away that night. Anne gave the talk and I didn't have a clue what she was about but it didn't matter. At the end, she invited people forward for prayer.

All the leaders of the church went to the front and they were each powerfully touched by the Spirit. I was completely dumb struck and suddenly I just knew, "There's a God! He really exists! He's here!" I was trembling with fear but I knew I had to come up to the front for prayer too.

Anne put her hand on me and said, "Come Holy Spirit" and the most incredible thing happened. I felt as if someone took two torches and put them into my eyes. I saw this incredible white light and my whole body, from my head to my toes, was bathed with bright white light. Liquid love was flooding into me and I kept saying over and over again, "I've met Jesus, I've met Jesus!"

I was so happy. That night I was leaping along the street and cars were passing me and I was shouting, "Yippee! This is JESUS, this is JESUS!"

I got home and started to collect all the nasty magazines, tarot cards, and immoral trash around my house and burnt all the stuff in my garden. I was laughing my head off and having a whale of a time. My boyfriend thought I was out of my mind but I told him I didn't care what he thought. "By the way," I said, "you and I are finished, kid." That was it—he left the next day. I wasn't sure what was happening to me yet but my life was beginning again and it felt incredible.

The next night, I heard a voice say over and over in my head, "You stupid thing. You stupid idiot. What do you think you're doing? There's no God. What did you dump your boyfriend for? Go and tell him that you want him back."

> **!**
> **Liquid love was flooding into me and I kept saying over and over again, "I've met Jesus, I've met Jesus!"**

I lay on the floor of my kitchen crying and pulling my hair out and then, in all that confusion and pain, I heard someone in the room say, "Michaela, do you love Me?" It was the most beautiful voice I'd ever heard and I knew it was Jesus.

The whole room was filled with His Spirit and His peace and I said, "Yes, Lord, I do." Then Jesus said, "Well, hold on tightly to Me now and I promise you with all My heart that I will take all your pain away." That night, in the solitude of my bedroom, I gave my life to Christ.

The next morning when I woke up, I knew beyond a shadow of a doubt that the old Michaela was dead and I was a brand new person.

I didn't feel any shame or guilt, self-hatred or addictions. I'd smoked 20 cigarettes a day for six years and I stopped then and there.

I was completely overflowing with Him. I was in ecstasy—I loved everybody and I would gaze with adoration at passersby. I was bursting with Jesus and I wanted to spend all my time on my knees praising God.

Since I've done Alpha, God has continued to heal me and He's made me feel more and more whole. I feel so forgiven. I was grieving for my baby after the course but God has even shown me a picture of my baby, that He was a boy, and even the color of his eyes. I know he's safe with Jesus.

Daniel is eight now and God has given me a new relationship with him that is so beautiful. We're the best of friends and have a great time together. My relationship with my mom had always been rocky and when I first told her I'd become a Christian, she couldn't cope with it. Then she got pneumonia and thought she was going to die. She'd always had a terrible fear of death. I reassured her that this life wasn't the end and that there was a heaven. I asked her to come on Alpha.

Mom came along and on the fifth talk of the course, she gave her life to Jesus. Afterward, she couldn't stop laughing and now she's a member of our church. Her fear of death has gone completely and our new relationship is so loving and strong.

I love verse five in Psalm 34, which says "Those who look to him are radiant; their faces are never covered with shame."

It's wonderful to have no shame and to be free of my past. I know Jesus, I know fullness of life in Him and I'm just so, so happy.

Michaela now works with Andrew Baguley as the church administrator of Helsby Methodist Church, Cheshire.

*"I was at the end of my rope and didn't know what to do.
I didn't want to kill myself. I just wanted it all to stop."*

The story of Bob Byrne

Between the ages of 17 and 21, Bob Byrne lived a life of violence, drug abuse, theft, and dishonesty. He ended up serving a two-year prison sentence for arson. Here he tells the story of how God changed his life forever.

I was born in Wimbledon and brought up in southwest London. I didn't come from a Christian family. My dad was Irish and I was taken to a Catholic church as a boy but it never really meant anything to me. My mother is Scottish and was ill when we were growing up so things were quite difficult at home. I became what is known as "behaviorally disturbed."

As a result of that I got expelled from all the schools I ever went to—four of them in all. I left school with no qualifications at the age of 15 and got a job making horses' saddles. One day I was walking past the Army careers office, dropped in and joined the Army. At the age of 16, I became 245 89133: Gunner Byrne, Royal Artillery.

I served a year in the Army during which time I served four short Army prison sentences for fighting. I got a dishonorable discharge—"services no longer required."

I returned to live with my parents for a short while and it was then that I got into taking drugs, crime, and was in trouble with the police loads of times. I ended up living in slums and really messing up. From the age of 17 to 21, I was wandering around the country involved in all sorts of crimes: drug dealing, violence—you name it, I got into it. I was involved in some pretty heavy stuff.

I didn't do heroin, but I used to do a lot of coke, acid, and sulfate.

I would have a joint for breakfast just to calm my nerves and then I would be on uppers all day. After that, things would get really out of hand.

I moved quite often because I used to get involved with some dangerous people. For some time I lived in Bristol dealing in drugs, but eventually I had to leave because I was going to get killed. Someone I worked for sent six people to my house and kicked the front door down. I jumped over the back fence. Large sums of money were involved and I had to leave quickly.

By the time I came back to London, I had completely lost touch with my parents, who had separated and moved away. I had no idea where they were.

I had nowhere to live so the first thing I did when I came back to London was to go to the home of a woman who had been a teacher of mine. She wasn't there, but I was met by her roommate and I sat waiting for her smoking dope and talking to the roommate.

When she came back she was a little bit annoyed to see me sitting smoking in her apartment. I was quite surprised because she had never objected in the past. It turned out that she had become a Christian.

She let me live on her sofa. She also introduced me to some Christian friends of hers who spoke to me about Christianity. I believed that Jesus Christ was God but I couldn't understand what it had to do with me because I was rotten and they were all nice, middle class people who wore suits. I did go to church for a short while. I tried to be religious, but it was short lived.

I managed to make contact with my family again. I found my sister by going to her school. I took her home on the back of my motorbike and found my mother that way.

Later, I moved to Leatherhead in Surrey, and got a job working with disabled students where a room went with the job. It was crazy and there were a lot of drugs about. While there, I was involved in burning down a building when high on drugs for which I became wanted by the police.

We had been on a night out during which I had been thrown through the window of a wine bar and I had been bottled—hit with a bottle. On the way home we tried to steal a car but that went wrong. Then we burned down this building causing $320,000 worth of damage.

I was caught by the police and released on bail. Then I ran off and went on the run. It was absolute madness for three or four months. I did untold frauds just to survive.

I ran off to Oxford where I began to sell drugs to students. I was on the run from the police for arson, for malicious wounding, and various other things. While I was there, I overdosed myself on drugs.

I was found by a Christian woman who took me to a hospital. While the doctor was pumping out my stomach I noticed that she was wearing a little silver fish on her lapel. I can't explain it but all I could think about was this little fish.

She told me it was a Christian symbol and that Jesus loved me. During that night I was at the end of my rope and I didn't know what to do. I didn't want to kill myself. I just wanted it all to stop. The next day the doctors came on their rounds and, as they were all going out, my doctor came running back and said, "I was praying for you last night and God told me to give you this." She dropped this card onto the bed and it was a little poem called Footprints. I read it and started crying.

Later, Heather, the Christian woman who had taken me to the hospital, came to visit and asked what I was going to do. I said, "I

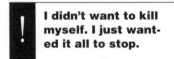

I didn't want to kill myself. I just wanted it all to stop.

am going to give myself up to the police." She said, "I will drive you back."

On the way down on the highway, we stopped at a gas station and she read through a little booklet with me called *Journey into Life*. We got to the end, where there was a prayer for anyone who wanted to ask God into their life. She said, "Do you want to pray this prayer?"

I thought, *If there is a Jesus and He does love me then I want to know that love.* I was empty inside. So I prayed the prayer, and genuinely asked God into my life. The woman told me God had forgiven me and given me a new start.

I was semi-literate. I was an alcoholic. I was a drug user. And my life was a complete mess. But I still believe God gave me a new start that day.

The courts understandably didn't quite see it like that and I got two years in prison. I served my term in Pentonville, Wandsworth, Highpoint and Brixton. I arrived in prison pretty well illiterate and it was while I was there that I learned to read and write properly. I was locked up 23 hours a day, during which time I just stayed in my cell. My mom and my sister came to visit me once while I was in prison.

Nevertheless, some of my best times as a Christian were when I was in prison. I had no problems whatsoever. People were a bit violent and stuff—but I read the Bible all the time. It was absolutely brilliant.

Once I ended up in the punishment block for two days. Someone attacked me and I ended up having a fight. I was in a strip cell. I had a blanket and no clothes. The bed was a concrete slab on the floor. The one thing I had in the punishment block at Wandsworth prison was a Bible. That was the one thing I was allowed and that was the one thing I wanted.

When I came out, God started to deal with some of the things that were messing up my life. It had been a lot easier to be a Christian in prison than out of prison.

I studied social sciences and wanted to be a social worker. I tried to go to a church in Wimbledon but they didn't want anything to do with me because I was an ex-con.

I moved to Clapham and that is when I got into contact with St. Mark's, Battersea Rise [*a church "planted" from Holy Trinity Brompton in 1987*]. I was invited to a newcomers' supper party. I was in a really nice house. I thought, *The only time I have ever been in a house like this was when I was robbing it.*

Although God had given me a new start, it took years to overcome some of the problems I had. It was through the love of Christians—particularly at St. Mark's—that I learned to be free, to live the freedom that God has given me in Christ, and for all the anguish and hurts of the past to leave me.

I started attending the Alpha course and felt really cared for in the small group. It was the first time since I had come out of prison that any Christians had bothered about me. This Christian thing I had signed up for started to make sense. Alpha grounded me in the basics of the Christian faith.

It was through going to St. Mark's and doing the first Alpha course that I really started to come to grips with who I was as a Christian. That is how the foundation of my faith was built upon.

I had an apartment near Clapham Common and I started organizing "open house" parties after church. We would have spaghetti, bologna, and curry and lots of people came.

A little while later I was taken on the staff of St. Mark's. I was given more responsibility in the church and gradually, over a period of four years, became involved in leading home groups, leading services, and preaching.

I then decided to get ordained. I got through the nightmare of the selection process somehow and went to Oak Hill Theological College.

A couple of years ago, when my mom was working for an old people's home owned by the Salvation Army, her friends there invited her to an Alpha course and she went along. One day, some time later, I went to see her for lunch and she told me that she had become a Christian. I had had nothing to do with it—apart from praying. It was wonderful and very moving for me.

For some years, I lost touch with my youngest sister, Maggie, who had emigrated to Australia with her two sons, Matthew and Jason, after being involved in a painful divorce. She had been heavily into drugs and the New Age and had dabbled in the occult at rock festivals while living on the road.

I had no idea where she had gone. All I could do was pray, which I did with a friend named Malin. At one point during our prayer time, Malin had a "picture" of Maggie and her sons returning home.

In early 1997, I received a letter from Maggie out of the blue. In it she wrote how she and the boys had ended up living on an organic farm in the outback about 100 miles from Perth. The farm was owned by an Australian folk singer Maggie had met at the Glastonbury Festival.

She wrote to say that she had started an Alpha course using the videos of Nicky Gumbel's talks. She said, "Before, I thought there was no hope. But now I have opened my life to God and He's changing me. . . I am sorry for doing the things that I have done that have upset you. . ."

It was an incredible shock. I just sat at my desk and wept for an hour.

Maggie and her sons were baptized in Australia and became members of the little outback church near their home. They are now back in England and God is working in her life.

The cross is the most important thing in my life. Before I became a Christian I was lost. I didn't know how to live my life. I have been stabbed in the stomach with a screwdriver, smacked over the head with an iron bar, and have had five stitches in my mouth and ten in my head. I have been stabbed through the wrist with a bottle, and have done those sorts of things to other people. Before, I lived those hurts every day of my life but now God has taken those hurts away from me one at a time.

My favorite hymn is "Amazing Grace." It is an incredible feeling to be saved from where I have been. It is so precious because you know how lost you were. But I also know that everybody else is lost as well.

I see people's lostness even though they might dress better, behave better, or live respectable lives. Their lostness is in terms of their relationship with God.

I see people from all walks of life who don't know God and I know that is the most precious thing that they could possibly find. I long for them to find it because I know how wonderful it has been for me.

Bob Byrne is now ordained in the Church of England. He is a curate in Tonbridge, Kent, where he lives with his wife, Debra, and two young daughters.

> "Seek your happiness in the LORD,
> and he will give you your heart's desire."
> *Psalm 37:4*

2

"I had no intention of making any real commitment to Jesus Christ because my relationship with Sila was far and away the most important thing in my life."

The story of Nicky and Sila Lee

Nicky Lee and Alison (known as "Sila") Callander had been in love for more than a year when they decided to give their lives to Jesus Christ during a mission at Cambridge University, where Nicky was a student. Their decision was to have a profound impact upon their relationship.

I was standing in line to get on the ferry at Swansea docks when I became fascinated by a girl trying to take a British sticker off the car immediately in front. I sat and watched her for some time. Then some great friends who were going on vacation to the same area of Ireland spotted me as they walked back toward their car from across the docks. It turned out that it was their car in front of mine and they introduced this girl to me. She was a school friend of one of the daughters of the family. It was Sila.

She was just 17 and I was a very mature 18 year old with a driver's license! I was in my battered old green Mini going on vacation with my family to southern Ireland. She had been removing the sticker because the father in the family is a Brigadier in the British Army and it was not a good idea at the time to display the fact that you were British, due to the troubles in the north. The moment I saw her I was smitten. It was love at first sight.

We ended up spending two weeks in vacation cottages next door to each other in southwest Ireland. I had fallen madly in love with her, but didn't say anything. I hardly dared believe that she might feel anything for me at all, but I tried to be with her as often as possible. Then, two days before the two week vacation was over, I plucked up the courage to tell her— and found to my astonishment that Sila had similar feelings. I could hardly believe it.

At that time, Sila still had another year to go at school—at Wycombe Abbey in Buckinghamshire —and I was trying to enter Cambridge, studying mainly from home.

Sila used to be involced in social services on Thursday afternoons and that proved to be a perfect opportunity to meet. The school was conveniently about 20 miles from my home. She would walk out of the school gates and up High Street in her school uniform. I would drive along in my old green Mini and, checking that there were no staff looking, would open the door. Sila would jump in and we would roar off.

We would often have a picnic in the fields and go for long walks and then I would drop her back. Sila would have her trousers under her uniform. Flared jeans were the fashion then, so they were easy to roll up under her skirt. This went on for a term, at least once a week.

I was offered a place at the university and had nine months before going up to Cambridge. Sila had exams to take and it was clear to both of us that she probably wouldn't pass them if I was still in the country, so I went off to Africa for six months.

Africa was fascinating and wonderful, but secretly I was longing to get back to England to see Sila. I would write to Sila from Africa every week during the six months I was there. I had organized for Sila to write to me in the capital cities of all the countries I was going through, from Ethiopia down to South Africa. Her letters were sent poste restante—to a central box in a city's main post office. I got letters in Addis Ababa and Nairobi and then Dar es Salaam and Zomba. I told Sila not to write to Mozambique because I was rather uncertain whether I would be able to go into the capital. I suggested she write to South Africa. I didn't specify which city. We had just agreed that it would be the capital city in each country.

It took me several weeks to get from Zomba to Johannesburg. It was very exciting going into the post office because I hadn't had a letter from Sila for weeks. I rushed in, but there was no letter. I was devastated. The next day I started to hitchhike to Cape Town because I thought she must have written to Cape Town and I had a cousin there. It took about two days to get there. As soon as I arrived, I rushed to the post office and got there just before it closed. I asked if there were any letters for Lee. There were hundreds of letters for Lee— there must be a big Chinese community in Cape Town—and in the end I found there was one for me. But it was from my mother! My mother is the most wonderful letter writer and I adored her letters, but this time it made my heart sink.

I went to the post office every day for the first couple of weeks, but there was no letter. After that I began to go twice a week, then once a week. I stayed there for about a month. I began to wonder if Sila's affection had cooled off because of the time I had been away. I started to think that perhaps I would stay in South Africa as long as I could and go back just before I started school. I wasn't in a hurry to get back if Sila wasn't interested in me anymore.

Then I decided to go back to Johannesburg and check once more. When I got there, I went back to the post office and there was a letter from Sila. I had just missed it on my previous visit. She had finished her exams so that same day I went to the travel agent and booked the first available flight home.

When I got back, I called Sila and said I was coming to visit her that very day. I went over to her school right away.

It was very much against the rules. Sila had two weeks left at school and I took her out on a Saturday evening. We had an arrangement with a friend that she would leave the library window open so that Sila could climb back in. By eleven o'clock, Sila wasn't back. We were still at the pub talking. The friend at school, Penny, who had invited Sila to come to Ireland, became concerned and went down to check that the library window hadn't been closed. At that moment, Penny ran into her house mistress just as Sila started climbing in the window.

She was caught red-handed and hauled before the headmistress the next day, rather expecting to be expelled. In the end she was grounded and wasn't allowed to leave the school. Because I had only seen her once since my six months in Africa, I was desperate to see her again. The only time visitors were allowed in was for chapel on Sunday. So I went to her chapel service on a Sunday and managed to get ten minutes with her at the end. I was even introduced to the headmistress!

That October I went up to Trinity College, Cambridge, where at first I felt quite desolate. The only person I knew who was coming up to the same college was a very good friend I had at school called Nicky Gumbel. There are over 1,000 people in Trinity College, so the chances of finding myself anywhere near him were remote. I went to the porter's lodge to see which room Nicky had.

Incredibly I found he was in the very next room to mine. I was in S1 Whewell's Court and he was in S2. I rushed back to my room just as he arrived.

He had been living in London up till then and had a stack of invitations to parties in London. For the first two weeks he spent more time on the train going back and forth to London than he spent in lectures. After a couple of weeks he decided that it would be better to spend more time in Cambridge and threw the whole pile of invitations into the trash, much to my delight.

During my first week at Cambridge, I met someone named John Hamilton, who was at Ridley College studying theology. He had come around visiting the "Freshers" who had just arrived for their first year. He knocked on my door and invited me to come to a talk. I was fascinated by the way he talked about a personal relationship with Jesus Christ. It had never occurred to me that God wanted to relate to us in a personal way. We had been to church rarely as a family and I always thought of God as a very mysterious spiritual being.

I liked John so I went along with him one Sunday evening to hear a talk given by a Christian speaker. I was fascinated by it and at the same time very threatened. I started playing squash with John, and we would see each other about once a week.

Some three weeks later, Nicky Gumbel said to me, "If any of those 'born-again Christians' come anywhere near your room, don't let them in. Talk to them through a crack in the door because if you let them in you won't be able to get rid of them."

He said he had met some people in America who called themselves "born-again Christians." He didn't know that I often used to go to these talks on a Sunday evening. I had no intention of making any real commitment to Jesus Christ, however, because my relationship with Sila was far and away the most important thing in my life.

By now we had known each other for 16 months. When I went up to Cambridge we started sleeping together, which seemed the natural, obvious thing to do. We were anticipating getting married to each other one day. We were deeply in love and deeply committed to each other. But I somehow knew that if I was to make a commitment to Jesus Christ and start this personal relationship with Him that I was hearing about, it would mean stopping sleeping together. There was a fear that God might take Sila away from me, that He might not want the relationship to continue.

Sila often came up from London on the weekends and I would never go to the Christian talk on a Sunday evening if she was still around. I was very attracted, yet very threatened at the same time.

Sometimes I couldn't face seeing John Hamilton because I knew that every time we would meet, at some point in our conversation we would talk about Christianity. Occasionally I can remember seeing him coming toward my rooms and hiding under my desk until the knocking stopped and I heard his footsteps fading away again.

In my second term a man called David MacInnes came to do a mission—a series of talks over 10 days—in a huge hall in Cambridge. John Hamilton invited me to go on the first evening. It was a Monday evening and we arrived late. We sat right at the back. I felt as though I was miles away from David MacInnes. Yet I had never heard anyone speak with more power in all my life. I knew that what David was speaking about was the power of love.

The following day John asked me to go again and I declined. But without John knowing, I went by myself. By then, the evidence was stacking up that what I was hearing was the truth.

When I got back to my room that night, I wrote down my impressions from the talk. At the end of that I wrote a prayer that went, "God, if You are there—and I think You are—I think that Jesus Christ is the Son of God and did rise from the dead and I need to make a commitment to You. But I don't think I have the strength to do so unless You convince Sila as well." The next day I drove down to London to see Sila. We were going out to see a movie and before going in we were sitting together in the car when I tried to explain to her what I had been hearing and thinking over the last six months about Christianity.

I said to her, "I think I am beginning to understand what it means to be a Christian. It means having a personal relationship with Jesus Christ." Sila was terribly enthusiastic and she said, "That sounds so exciting! I would love to do that!"

My heart sank. I thought, *She doesn't know what it means. She hasn't got a clue that we will have to stop sleeping together and it might mean the end of our relationship.* I was very depressed.

That Friday night Sila came up to Cambridge. I went to meet her at the train and suggested to her that we should go and hear David MacInnes. It was a very odd thing for us to do on a Friday night, but she agreed.

That evening I hardly listened to what David said at all. I was simply watching Sila's reaction. I could tell that Sila was responding just as I had done over the past six months—very drawn and compelled by what she was hearing, but very threatened by it. She began to realize what the implications were for our relationship. That night we talked for a long time.

The next day we went again to hear David MacInnes. Each evening David said, "If there are people who want to pray to ask Jesus Christ to come into their lives, they should stay behind and I shall explain to them exactly what it means to start this relationship with Jesus." Sila and I didn't say anything to each other, but we both knew that this was what we had to do and wanted to do.

We stayed behind with about 50 others. After talking briefly to us, David led us in a prayer that Jesus would come in to fill our lives as we committed ourselves to following Him. On the way out, I saw a friend of mine, Steve Ruttle, who I knew was a Christian and I said to him, "That was one of the most amazing evenings of my life."

Stephen then said at once, "Is it 'yes' or 'no' then?"

I knew that everything hung on the next word I said. It seemed like ages passed and then I heard myself say, "Yes."

At that moment I knew that it was not only true, but it made sense of everything else in my life. It was the most extraordinary moment.

The best way I can describe it is as though all the different parts of my life were like a jigsaw puzzle: my past, my relationship with Sila, my reading English, my being at the university, everything. It was as though suddenly all the jigsaw pieces fell into place at that moment. I knew that Jesus Christ was the key to it all.

That night when Sila and I went back to my room, we knew that we had to wait until we were married before we made love to

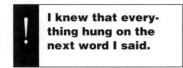

I knew that everything hung on the next word I said.

each other again (although nobody told us). But we thought it would be fine to sleep in the same bed. We talked and cried quite a bit that night wondering what the effect on our relationship would be. Our fear was that God might separate us.

We did realize over the coming months that it was going to be very hard to sleep together in the same bed if we weren't going to make love! So after a few weeks, I remember another very tearful evening when I suggested it might be better if I slept on the floor and Sila slept on the bed.

Then a few weeks—or perhaps months—later, we thought that it wasn't helpful if we slept in the same room. I should sleep in the next door room. That was another tearful night. A few months later we decided that it was better if, when Sila came up to Cambridge, she went to stay with some friends and not stay in my rooms at all.

It was a process and I was amazed at how God took us from stage to stage. I think we knew it was God speaking to us. The thing that we discovered as much as anything after we had become Christians was that there was a new freedom in our relationship—a closeness that we had never experienced before and a greater trust in each other. We both started going to church. Sila was usually in Cambridge on a Sunday and so we would go to the Round Church together.

About eight months after that Saturday evening with David MacInnes, we both independently began to feel that we had to put our relationship into God's hands. It was very hard for us to know if we had really done so when we were seeing each other all the time. In addition to that, it was very hard to control the physical side of our relationship.

> There was a new freedom in our relationship—a closeness that we had never experienced before.

One weekend, we discovered that we had come to the same conclusion independently of each other—that if we were really to trust God with the future, we needed to spend some time apart. We felt that God would show us over that time whether our relationship was to continue and go on to marriage.

So very early one Monday morning at the beginning of October, I waved good-bye to Sila at Cambridge Station. We had agreed that we wouldn't see each other or talk on the telephone until Christmas, although we would write letters.

It was like a scene from the film *Dr. Zhivago*. It was 6:30 A.M. on a beautiful autumn morning, with a carpet of mist that hadn't yet lifted. Sila was waving good-bye to me out the window and I wondered if I would ever see her again. I walked back through the still deserted streets of Cambridge feeling as low as I can ever remember feeling in my life.

After eight months as Christians, I think we had come to realize that God really did have the best plan for our lives. He wasn't a spoilsport who was wanting to stop us from enjoying ourselves. I decided that because Sila was living in Parsons Green, I wouldn't go near London because it would be too painful to be there and not see Sila.

A week later, I drove with three friends to my old school in Berkshire to play a football match. We didn't need to go through London at all, which was a great relief to me. But as we drove back after the match, the friend who was driving suddenly said to my horror, "If you don't mind I have to drive by my home in Kensington to pick something up from my mother."

I was absolutely horrified, but I didn't say anything to him. I thought, *It won't take very long. I'll keep my head down.*

The friend dropped us on High Street Kensington, near Barkers, and said, "I will pick you up here in 40 minutes," and drove off. It was pouring rain and we stood on the pavement trying to decide what we were going to do when I looked up and there, about 50 yards away, walking down the pavement toward me, was Sila.

I abandoned my two friends without a word of explanation and ran towards her. Then she saw me. She had galoshes on because of the rain and started running toward me. We flung our arms around each other on the pavement of High Street Kensington and I remember swinging her round and round. I shouted back to my friends not to wait for me. I wouldn't be coming back. Sila and I went off together.

Sila was at art college at the time and went to a weekly Bible study group run by a Christian organization called the Arts Center Group, which unbeknownst to me met just behind High Street Kensington. Traveling by bus, she had gotten stuck in heavy traffic, so she decided to get off the bus and walk the last 500 yards. That was when she saw me.

It was one of the most exciting moments in my life. We felt that if God could cause us to meet in this extraordinary way when we were doing our best to avoid each other, He was easily capable of showing us over the next 10 weeks whether He intended that we should spend the rest of our lives together. So there was another tearful parting, but it was much easier this time. We knew we could trust God.

We didn't hold out quite till Christmas, but we did make it to the end of the term. It was wonderful to have that time of writing letters to each other and our friendship, knowledge, and trust of each other grew over those weeks.

By the end of the term there was no doubt in our minds that God wanted us to be together and that we would then be able to make serious plans for getting married. I still had another year and a half at the university, but it was a wonderful time with Sila spending most weekends up at Cambridge. We grew as Christians. We grew in our relationship with each other and our love for each other.

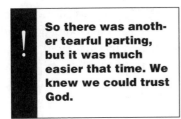

So there was another tearful parting, but it was much easier that time. We knew we could trust God.

It was always a struggle to keep the physical side of our relationship within proper bounds but we knew that it was right to wait until we were married before we slept together again.

I planned to take a teacher training course after leaving Cambridge and Sila was still at art college. We talked about marriage but, being students, we thought we'd have to wait another two years.

In January of my last year at Cambridge I talked late into the night with a good friend, Ken Costa, about the future. I remember Ken saying to me, "Do you have to wait till you have both stopped being students? You both need to be supported anyway and it won't be more expensive if you are married."

As we talked I began to realize that it would be possible to be married while we were still students. I went back to my room at about two o'clock in the morning and wrote Sila a long letter asking her to marry me and explaining why I thought we could do so while we were both still students.

I put it in a letter because I thought I had a better chance of Sila saying yes, as she would have more time to think about all the reasons why it was a good idea. I mailed it and then waited for a reply. The next day I got a telegram from Sila saying, "I would love to with all my heart."

I went up to Scotland where Sila's home was and asked her father. He said, "Yes." I talked to my parents as well because we needed their help in supporting us for our first year of marriage. I was just 22 and Sila was 20.

We were married on July 17, 1976 at St. Andrew's, Callander, near Sila's home. There was no doubt in our minds that God had brought us together. Far from drawing us apart, God has increased our love for each other and taught us how to express that love in practical ways. We are so grateful to have Him at the center of our marriage, giving a strength to our relationship far beyond anything we could have on our own.

> "I look back and see so clearly God's hand
> in our lives."

Sila Lee tells the story from her own point of view

I grew up on the edge of the Highlands in the most beautiful part of Scotland. It was an idyllic childhood, although at the time I thought it was slightly boring because I was an extrovert and liked people. Yet there was nobody to see all day except the mailman and the milkman.

I grew up believing in God. My father has a very strong faith and he and my mother used to pray a short prayer with us as children before we went to sleep. My father has been to church every Sunday for as long as I can remember.

I was a bit of a rebel, and decided I didn't want to get confirmed with everyone else at school, but after a year I changed my mind. So

I took confirmation classes.

I remember that as a significant time. The classes were taught by the headmistress and I recall her saying, "It is an outward physical sign of the inward spiritual truth."

I also remember the bishop who confirmed us gave us the verse John 10:10: "I have come that you might have life, and life in all its fullness." I never forgot that verse. I used to remind myself of it often.

One of my best friends was Penny Somerville and she said to me when I was 16, "Come and stay with us in Ireland." I had no idea this would change my life for ever. Their family was Anglo-Irish and came from southwest of Cork. They used to go there for their summer vacations and she said, "You'll really like it because it is so like Scotland and we spend the whole time outside in boats, sailing, fishing, swimming, and barbecuing."

And she added, "There is also a wonderful family called the Lees. They have just bought the house next door to ours."

I was very excited about going. She told me all about the members of the Lee family, as well as cousins and friends. It sounded like absolute bliss to me—all those people!

I traveled with her family down to Swansea to catch the ferry to Ireland. When we got to Swansea, we parked in the line for the ferry. Penny pointed out a little green Mini driving toward us and said, "Look, there's Nicky."

Then she and her parents saw Nicky's parents in another car and went over to say hello. I was left peeling off the GB sticker because I didn't know them.

At this point this little green Mini drew up behind me. I looked up as this guy got out of the car. I was completely bowled over. Instantly I felt, "I really am attracted to him!"

He had on a black hat and a white shirt and was really tan. I thought, *He's fantastic!*

For two weeks Penny and I talked a lot but I never let on even to Penny, my closest friend, that I had fallen madly in love with Nicky.

We spent an amazing two weeks sailing, swimming, climbing rocks, and other similar activities. I realized that Nicky loved the same things as me and so I competed with him at everything to attract his attention! Forty-eight hours before I left to go back to Scotland we discovered that we both felt exactly the same for each other and that was wonderful.

From the moment that he first kissed me at the end of our Irish vacation, I knew that I would spend the rest of my life with him. I remember lying in bed in Ireland the night after he kissed me and thinking, *I want to be married to this man.* Since then I have never looked at another man in the same way.

Back at school, Penny and I used to rush down to the mail boxes every morning. We often read each other's letters.

On one of the first days of the new term after the summer, Penny looked at one of my letters and said, "That is Nicky's writing!"

I said, "Let's open it and read it." So I opened it and pulled out the letter and started reading. It began, "My dearest darling Sila. I love you more than words . . ."

Penny said, "Sila! I didn't know he felt like that about you."

She was very surprised but as excited as I was about it. I think it cemented our friendship forever. She is still my closest friend.

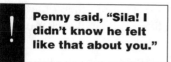

Penny said, "Sila! I didn't know he felt like that about you."

I still have all the letters Nicky wrote to me from Africa. I was doing English Lit., which Nicky had just done, so the letters were full of quotes from Shakespeare and Donne. Very helpful for my exams! Our friendship deepened as other aspects of our characters emerged through that letter-writing time.

At school, I used to climb into my wardrobe at night after "lights out" with the bedside light on and sit and write letters for hours at night to Nicky in Africa.

People said to me at school, "You really mustn't pin your hopes on this relationship. Nicky's going off to Africa and he is bound to meet somebody else. This is just a schoolgirl romance." But I knew that no matter how long he was gone, I would still love him when he came back.

The mix-up with my letters to Africa was awful. I wrote to Cape Town but I don't know what happened. Maybe the letter got lost.

Nicky had said he wouldn't come back from Africa until my term had finished. Then one day after I had finished my exams someone came running through the corridor shouting, "Sila, Sila, Nicky's on the phone."

I thought, *My goodness, he's on the telephone from Africa.* So I bolted down to the telephone and this voice said, "It's me. I'm here. I'm in England—can I come and see you?"

I thought, *I can't believe this! He's back!*

And he said, "I've come back because I couldn't bear to be away from you any longer." It was an amazing moment. That evening we went out to dinner and I got caught climbing back in through a window . . .

My father was very upset when I was grounded, but my parents really liked Nicky from the moment they met him, so I think that eased the situation.

When Nicky went up to Cambridge, I spent more time at Cambridge than I did at my secretarial college in London. It was then that Nicky and I started sleeping together. I knew my father's views on sex before marriage because he had often spoken about it when referring to "the young of today." He had what I thought of then as a very "traditionalist" view on the subject, which I disagreed with. However, deep down inside I knew it was wrong but I did not know why.

I justified sleeping together by saying, "When you love somebody so much that you want to spend the rest of your life with him and you think that you are going to get married, then it's OK. It is totally different than promiscuous relationships where you jump in and out of bed with different people. You're committed. You're in love. It is the ultimate way of showing that you love somebody and you want to give yourself to him." I convinced myself this reasoning would do, because I wanted it to.

I never doubted God and His existence. Every so often Nicky and I would go off to early morning communion at Trinity College Chapel—a totally traditional church service.

In a sense I think I felt I could earn my way into heaven—sometime in the future when I was older and more serious! But my belief in God simply had no effect on my lifestyle. It was in a separate compartment and I thought it was fine to keep it that way.

We had the most fantastic fun that first term at Cambridge with Nicky Gumbel and the other three "Nickys" who were there (there were five Nickys who were all great friends). We went to parties the whole time and spent quite a lot of time drinking!

I remember very well the time during our second term when Nicky took me out to dinner and started talking to me about Christianity. I thought, *Yes, that sounds great! I believe in God anyway.* I had no idea of the implications of what he was talking about, and looking back on it I hadn't understood at all.

When I arrived in Cambridge that weekend he took me straight to hear David MacInnes. I was amazed by what I heard. What had happened for Nicky over a period of about six months happened to me in the space of about 24 hours.

I was absolutely fascinated by what David said. It just made so much sense. I had never heard anybody talk about Jesus Christ like this in all the years I had been to school chapel and all the years I had been to church with my father in Scotland. Nobody had ever said you could have a relationship with Jesus Christ.

For me relationship was everything and suddenly this was making sense. That Friday night, we talked long into the night with Nicky Gumbel who, at that stage, was extremely suspicious of what we were up to.

On Saturday, we went back to hear David MacInnes again. He talked about the Cross. It was a revelation and made so much sense. I kept saying to myself: "Why did nobody ever tell me before why Jesus died on the cross?"

It was as if everything I had ever known came together and made sense—not just theologically and intellectually, but also emotionally and spiritually. Everything made sense when the Cross was explained.

We both got up without hesitation when David asked if anybody wanted to respond. David led us in a prayer with lots of other people.

As we walked away, it was as if my life up to that point had been like a black and white still photograph and suddenly now it was in glorious technicolor, a moving motion picture. It was that much of a radical change.

It is interesting that some people say Christianity is a crutch. As for myself, before I became a Christian, I felt like the happiest person in the world. I had grown up in a wonderful family. I had wonderful parents. I had a tremendous time at school. I had then met and fallen in love with an amazing man with whom I thought I was going to spend the rest of my life. I was about to go to art college, which I wanted to do. I felt fulfilled and happy. (One of the few things I felt guilty about deep down was sleeping with Nicky.)

When I heard about the Cross, I think I was beginning to understand the truth of the verse in John 10:10 "I have come that you might have life and life in all its fullness." I saw for the first time that perhaps I hadn't quite gotten the full picture and my life wasn't entirely what God would like it to be. I was not looking for a crutch, but the Holy Spirit revealed to me my need for a relationship with

God through Jesus. In the next weeks and months, that is what God started to unfold. It was so incredibly exciting.

That first night after we prayed with David MacInnes we went back to Nicky's room. It was amazing but we both knew that we couldn't sleep together again. We never made love together again from that time until the night we were married.

Nevertheless, it was an agonizing night. I remember crying and crying because I felt that here was God whom I knew I wanted to love and give my life to—but He was dividing Nicky and me. It didn't add up. Jonathan Fletcher [*who was the curate at the Round Church in Cambridge*] was an amazing support and friend to us. Jonathan must have known we had been sleeping together, but he never once tackled us on it. He left it to the Holy Spirit to do His work of conviction. I know He prayed for us every day in those early days.

I went back to my apartment and told Penny all about my newfound relationship with Jesus Christ, and she thought it was wonderful and wanted to become a Christian too. I called the curate at St. Paul's Church in Onslow Square, whose name I had been given by Jonathan Fletcher in Cambridge, and said, "Could we come to your Bible study and could I bring my roommate?"

We went to a Bible study in a room that coincidentally is now our dining room and Penny gave her life to Jesus Christ that night. It was wonderful! She is now also married to a clergyman.

In the next weeks and months it was incredibly exciting discovering a relationship with Jesus together. There was very good teaching in Cambridge and we—Nicky, Nicky Gumbel and I—used to go every Saturday night to the Union to hear a talk by a Christian speaker.

But I began to realize that my faith and my relationship with Jesus Christ were totally entangled with my love for Nicky, which was deepening and growing all the time. My whole life revolved around Nicky. I used to go to Cambridge whenever I could.

One week in London, I felt God saying, "I want you to put Me first over and above Nicky." I thought the only answer was for me and Nicky to spend some time apart so that I could grow in my relationship with Jesus by myself.

That was very hard and I wondered how I would ever be able to explain it to Nicky because it would be so hurtful. I thought, *He will never understand this.*

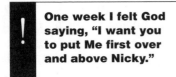

One week I felt God saying, "I want you to put Me first over and above Nicky."

I went to Cambridge and was anxious all weekend. Eventually on Sunday afternoon I thought, *I am going to have to talk to him about it.*

When I finally said it, Nicky told me that God had been saying exactly the same thing to him! It was an incredible "coincidence" and a huge relief.

It was the last thing in the whole world that I wanted to do, to spend any time apart from Nicky. Yet, I knew that was what God was asking me to do. The choice was obedience to God or doing what I wanted to do. Either you do what God says or you do what you want and you feel.

Looking back on it now, it was the most incredible lesson in obedience that I have ever learned. I think God knew that I needed to learn it in this radical way to stand me in good stead for the rest of my life.

We both decided that this was what God wanted, even though we didn't. We believed that God's plans were best for us and we would put our lives into His hands.

I was supposed to go back to London on Sunday night, but I said to Nicky, "I just can't go. I absolutely can't go. I need to stay here for one more night and I'll go in the morning."

That Monday morning was awful. It was just like *Dr. Zhivago.* Tears were streaming down my face as the train drew out of Cambridge Station and I waved and thought, "I can't believe I am doing this. This is absolutely mad, but I believe this is God at work in our lives."

I went back to London and spent the next five days crying all the time. Penny thought I had gone completely mad. My sister thought so too and she said, "I just can't believe you are doing this. This is the most ridiculous thing you could ever do. Nicky is the most wonderful man. What do you mean you are not going to see him?"

The following Thursday I was planning to go to a Bible study at the Arts Center Group. It was pouring rain and I thought, *I don't feel like going, but I need to do something.*

So I got on the bus and went up to High Street Kensington. The rain was pouring down and the traffic was terrible around Kensington Palace. I was on the top level of the bus and we were sitting in a traffic jam and hadn't moved for about five or ten minutes. I thought, *This is hopeless.* Then I felt this tremendous urge to get off the bus.

I went down the stairs and pushed my way through the people at the bottom and jumped off on to Kensington High Street. I turned in the direction of Barkers and had walked about five steps when suddenly there in front of me on the pavement I saw Nicky running towards me, about 20 yards away. I couldn't believe it!

We ran into each other's arms and he whirled me round and round and round. I remember screaming, "Nicky!" at the top of my voice.

At that moment I thought, *God, I will never doubt You again.*

As if in a flash of revelation I realized that I didn't need to worry about anything for the rest of my life—that God was a God who could do the impossible if we would just take the risk of trusting Him.

I knew with a tremendous conviction that Nicky and I were meant for each other, that God wanted us to get married and that I could trust God with everything, even with Nicky.

We did spend that time apart and I did grow in my own relationship with God. It was great having Nicky Gumbel around too. By now he and Nicky shared rooms and we learned fast that it was important for the two of us to be in an environment where we were not on our own for a long time without fear of disturbance. That was too strong a temptation. To be in such a situation presented too strong a temptation.

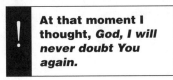

> At that moment I thought, *God, I will never doubt You again.*

At one stage, we planned to go on vacation together to Greece before we got married—on our own. We had some good advice not to go—and actually it never came off. I now realize we couldn't have done it. You can't walk into temptation like that.

I am so grateful that we didn't because it meant that we didn't sleep together again from the point we became Christians until our wedding. In all, it was about two and a half years between when we became Christians and when we were married.

We learned a lot during that time about relationships. The physical side of our relationship wasn't easy, but we learned why God's ways for us are best. We grew to understand why he created sex for a lifelong, committed, marital relationship. We learned the difference between lust and showing care and affection for each other. It was an important lesson to learn.

I look back and see so clearly God's hand on my life and on Nicky's life. I don't believe that there is an exclusive Mr. Right and a Miss Right—I don't believe that He puts a label on one person here and another person there.

I believe that God puts His hand on our lives and draws us to Himself through His love, and He sees how we respond, and as we do so His plans unfold.

I look back now and proclaim, "What an amazing God He is!"

Nicky Lee is now ordained and on the staff of Holy Trinity Brompton. He and Sila speak widely on the subjects of marriage and family life.

> "When anyone is joined to Christ, he is a new being;
> the old is gone, the new has come."
> *2 Corinthians 5:17*

3

"I had everything I ever wanted but I had lost my soul in the process."

The story of Nigel Skelsey

Nigel Skelsey quickly rose to his position as Photo Editor of a national newspaper, but felt he had "lost his soul in the process." He joined the HTB Alpha course in 1994 and wrote a letter to the course leader, Nicky Gumbel, about the effect it had had on his life. With his permission, the letter is reproduced here:

Dear Nicky,

I was going to start this letter by saying, "Just a short note to tell you what the Alpha weekend meant to me," but I'm afraid it's turned into a long note. Please bear with me, but it's something I feel I need to get down on paper.

In 1979 my father died of stomach cancer and it was at that time that my Christian faith went on the back burner, and for the last 15 years I haven't known why. It wasn't, as one might suppose, the question of suffering and a loving God. That wasn't a problem for me. I have subsequently found it to be far more deep-rooted than a moral dilemma.

For most of my life I have felt I've been a huge disappointment both to God and my parents.

When I left school I spent three years at theological college training to be a church minister with a genuine desire to be an evangelist— but I failed academically, ending up with the double burden of not only being looked upon by my parents as a failure but also, I felt, by God as well.

I decided to pursue a career in photography, which was a hobby of my father's, with the hope of winning my parents' approval, and I joined a publishing company as a gopher on a newly-launched photographic magazine. I had been there six months when my father took ill and eventually died. Just two weeks afterward the staff, on what was an ailing magazine, were sacked or left of their own volition. The gopher was the only one left and was promptly made editor by default. It was a success of sorts and something of which my father would have been incredibly proud. But he wasn't there to see it and I was devastated.

For 15 years there followed a faithless and obsessive pursuit of success for its own sake. Every time I achieved something I would scrap and start over again from scratch. I was like a child with building bricks. I would build a tower and shout, "Look, Dad!" before knocking it down and building another one to impress him with.

My career was like a roller-coaster. The ailing magazine, more by luck than judgment, given my inexperience, was turned round and within two years was the biggest selling monthly photographic magazine in the country. At the height of its success, and after only two years on the job, I left to join another magazine that was in a poor state. Within two years circulation was surging to the point of overtaking the first magazine. Once more success came quickly, but it wasn't enough and after another two years I put an end to that and decided to launch my own photographic magazine that within no time at all, became renowned around the world, picking up publishing awards along the way.

Another two years had gone by and I still wasn't satisfied, so in

1987 I decided that I wanted to be photo editor of a national newspaper. I had no experience in that particular industry and to all, bar the totally demented, it did not enter the realm of possibility. Since I was fast joining the ranks of the totally demented I didn't see the problem and within three years, at the grand old age of 37, I became the photo editor of the *Sunday Telegraph.*

Just before Christmas 1993 I turned 40 and, probably like many reaching that age, decided to reflect on what I had achieved and possibly where the next challenge lie. Forgetting the spiritual side— which was non-existent anyway—I was very satisfied. I had everything I had ever wanted in life: a fulfilling, well-paid job, a beautiful wife, two great sons and, at one point I'm embarrassed to say, a Porsche 911. But at what cost?

I discovered that my nickname at *The Telegraph* was "The Beast." Despite the affectionate undertones that many nicknames have, it told me something about myself that I didn't like. I also overheard someone else say that I was not truly happy unless I was at war with someone. They were right. In fact, if conflict didn't happen to come my way, I created it. Life had become a great battlefield.

Jesus said, "Love your neighbor as yourself," but my trouble was that deep down I hated myself and I hated my neighbor as myself. My motto was: "Forget revenge, get your retaliation in first!" I was like some aging prize fighter who doesn't know when to give up. Every single day of the last 15 years has been a brawl, only, unlike a boxing match, the bell never came at the end of each round. Worst of all I looked in the bathroom mirror one morning and saw reflected back someone I just didn't know anymore. Over the next few days the words of Jesus kept coming back to me, "What good will it be for a man if he gains the whole world, yet forfeits his soul?," and I realized that I had done just that. In my own little world I literally had everything I ever wanted but I had lost my soul in the process.

Then on New Year's Day a friend whom I hadn't seen for years came to dinner. What struck me was that he wasn't the person I used to know. Even though a Christian, my old friend was the most dreadful pessimist whose character I despised; the new version sitting in front of me was full of vigor, optimism, and genuine happiness. And he started to tell me about the great work that the Holy Spirit had done in his life. He went on to describe how he had felt like a failure all his life and how his father had been hugely disappointed in him and, without warning, I burst into inconsolable floods of tears at the dinner table: something "The Beast" was not prone to doing!

> **But my trouble was that deep down I hated myself and I hated my neighbor as myself.**

He was describing what was locked away deep in my subconscious and, although I didn't realize it, had been dominating my life all these years. Unruffled, he stood up and prayed over me and I felt the most extraordinary tingling sensation flooding through me, flushing out all the deep-rooted unhappiness that had slowly festered beneath the surface over the years.

I had experienced something I didn't understand, but which had a profound effect on me. I woke up the next morning like a man obsessed with a new ambition. I sensed God loved me and that I wasn't a write-off in His eyes. I was still heavily chained at the bottom of a deep dark prison, only someone had punched a hole in the wall and a chink of light was spilling in, giving me a taste of the freedom that was there if only I would grab a hold of it.

In the summer I had been on vacation in Switzerland and had read an article in a magazine I found about the Alpha course at Holy Trinity Brompton. The one thing that had stuck in my mind was how the work of the Holy Spirit was described as of paramount importance. I knew in my heart I had to have His power in my life at any cost so I found out where the church was, enrolled on the course and focused on the weekend. I felt like a dying man waiting for a life-saving operation. Never mind the weeks of pre-med, I just had to get into the operating room.

The weekend I had been waiting for, like a child waiting for Christmas, finally arrived . . . and I didn't want to go! I didn't realize what a spiritual battle I was about to experience. I lay in bed at the conference center on Friday night and went through an onslaught the like of which I have never experienced before and, I hope, never do again. Voices screamed in my head to get out, go home, I was making a fool of myself, God wouldn't do anything for me, I was beyond hope, I was a failure, etc. I tried to pray but I couldn't. I just lay there for what seemed like hours and got the biggest mauling of my life.

I woke up in the morning shattered. I looked at the schedule, saw that the third session (which I had identified as the main one) was at 4:30 P.M. and simply hung on like a marathon runner weaving his way up the final stetch with nothing but the finish line as the focus of his attention.

I'll never forget that final session. I felt as though I was torn in two. Halfway through I just couldn't stand it anymore. The prize was so near but we were getting there so slowly! I literally wanted to scream out, "Do it now! Do it now! I can't hold out any longer." I'm not exaggerating when I say I was in agony. Then God came, and oh, the relief.

> **The weekend I had been waiting for, like a child waiting for Christmas, finally arrived.**

Do you know, for the first time in my life I feel normal. It seems a strange thing to say but it keeps hitting me just how normal I feel! I also feel loved. I am accepted for who I am and I feel free. Terribly clichéd, isn't it? But I feel so free!

Yesterday I read some words of Paul in Philippians which express so deeply how I now feel about my "achievements" of the past 15 years: "But whatever was to my profit I now consider loss for the sake of Christ. What is more, I consider everything a loss compared to the surpassing greatness of knowing Christ Jesus my Lord, for whose sake I have lost all things. I consider them rubbish, that I may gain Christ and be found in him. . . . But one thing I do: Forgetting what is behind and straining towards what is ahead, I press on toward the goal to win the prize for which God has called me heavenward in Christ Jesus" (Phil. 3:7-9a, 13b).

I don't know what the future holds or where and how God will lead me; at the moment I'm just enjoying a honeymoon period! Which brings me to the point of this letter. Thank you for helping to bring to completion what was started on New Year's Day.

Regards,
Nigel

Nigel Skelsey is still Photo Editor of The Sunday Telegraph. *He has led groups at numerous Alpha courses at Holy Trinity Brompton as well as being a member of his local church, which he attends regularly with his family.*

> "It was like there was this wall up and God has knocked all the bricks out from the bottom of the wall and they came tumbling down."

The story of Steve Diddams

Police Officer Steve Diddams, a Chief Inspector in Croydon, Surrey, "didn't see any reason for religion." But when his Christian wife Kathy was sent one of the Alpha videos, Steve sat and watched it—and was gripped. He then went on an Alpha course at his wife's church and his perception of life changed. Here he describes what happened:

I was born in Hendon, North London, near the Police Academy. Although my parents were not regular churchgoers, they sent me to Sunday school at the local Methodist church. When I was 16, I joined the Royal Marines. As soon as I moved away, I suddenly started to question my belief. I realized I hadn't really had a faith. I think I had gone along with the crowd. I didn't argue against religion at that time, but I would have reacted badly to anyone who tried to come up and say, "Let's go to church" or "What are your beliefs?"

Soon afterward, I joined the police force. I started off at Bow Street and have served in most areas in my service. From Bow Street, I went into traffic. I was promoted and went to south east London. Then I went back into traffic in south London, then I got promoted again and went to Peckham, Streatham and Brixton. I was there during the second Brixton riot.

All the time I was pretty much a self-contained non-believer. I had met my wife, Kathy, within a year of joining the force. I met her in 1972. She has always been a Christian, but it was not until the last five years really that she has become a committed Christian, insofar as she has gone through a life-changing experience.

We were married in a church in 1976. I didn't really take a great part in what was going on. I was quite happy and didn't see any reason to have any form of religion. My wife was sad that I wasn't a Christian. When she went to church, I would stay at home. We were both shift-workers for some time. She was a nurse in hospital work, so she would go to church in the various places where we lived and I would have nothing to do with it. I don't think I even went along to Christmas carol services or to a christening—just weddings and funerals. I didn't want to take part in any services. I didn't see the need.

My wife and I would have long conversations. At the time of her uncle's death, a lot of things came together. She was deeply affected by his death and she went to church. She really started to get involved. She became a regular church attendee, and at that stage she was really trying to make an effort for me.

In September, 1995 we went on vacation to Dorset just as her church was doing a prayer walk back home. She decided to do her own prayer walk while on vacation, so, unbeknownst to me, we were going around to these churches and she was writing down what was happening to her while her friends were doing the same at home. I was completely oblivious to all this. Every time she went into a church and said, "I am just going to stay here for a little while," I would be standing outside thinking, "Oh come on! Let's get to the pub." When we came back, I noticed the radio was always switched to Premier [*a Christian radio station in London*]. Whenever I switched a tape on in the car, there was always a worship tape in there. There seemed to be books and pamphlets everywhere.

A year ago, I became ill with high blood pressure. I was off work for a few weeks. Kathy was getting quite upset, because she thought that I might die outside of faith. That was her concern. I didn't know this at the time, but she was praying with other members of the church for me to attend. After my illness, she said, "They have all been praying for you. Will you come to church one morning?" I went to the eight o'clock service . The vicar was Bob Callaghan, who was surprised to see me. I said, "Kathy suggested I come along to say 'thank you' for the prayers you have been saying for me." That must have been about January 1996. But the service meant nothing to me. Kathy tried to pin me down. "Why don't you believe?" she asked. I said, "I don't believe in life after death. I don't see the purpose of it, so therefore I can't be a Christian. I believe that there is a historical figure called Jesus and that He did good works. But I don't believe that He was the Son of God and that He was God. I don't believe in the supernatural aspects. And that is it. There is nothing that you are going to do to convince me otherwise."

Then one day she came back—this was around Easter last year— and said that the church was going to do Alpha. The vicar wanted to put the whole congregation through Alpha—some 80-plus people.

They weren't sure whether to use the videos or give their own talks, so they gave all the leadership group, including my wife, a tape each and said, "Take it back and see what you think of it." They did and the decision was that Bob Callaghan, the vicar, would do his own and not use the video tapes.

It just so happened that the tape we had was Tape One. I was quite interested in it, so I said to Kathy, "Get the other tapes. I want to run through this."

So I went through the tapes. I liked Nicky's style. You can tell he is an ex-lawyer. He has a brilliant use of the pregnant pause. I found some of it gut-wrenchingly emotional. It really had an effect on me. I was eager to go through all of them—some more than others.

I was doing it at home, just running through the tapes, some-times on my own and sometimes with Kathy. I went through the whole lot. Then Kathy said, "Well, come along to Alpha." And I said, "I will come along, but this has got to be the final time. If, at the end of the 10 weeks, I am not a Christian, then you have had your best shot and then let's leave it alone." I didn't say it cruelly like that but it was, "This is it. If I am not going to be a Christian after this, then I am never going to be a Christian. And will you agree to that?"

I can't remember if she agreed or not. She probably muttered something, but I don't think she would have agreed to it. She wouldn't have stopped.

I went along to the course along with 80 people, most of whom I had never met before. One of the churchwardens' daughters does catering and she produced an excellent meal—really good. The talks were excellent. The vicar did the talk. They were personalized and he brought in anecdotes from Temple Hill, which is largely a council estate.

Everybody from the church was doing Alpha. Some were in their seventies and some in their late teens. Some people had moved out of the estate, but it was largely the local people. I think I was the only non-Christian that went there and I was very much aware that I was being targeted. They were very good about it—never overt or anything. It was always, "How's it going, Steve?"

The talk that particularly struck me was "Why did Jesus die?" That was near the beginning. I had no idea why He had died. It was just so enormous. I have always been a very unemotional person, rationalizing everything. I look for systems and proofs in everything, but here I was being emotionally affected by the presentations. We came to the Holy Spirit weekend. We did it in the church: Friday evening, all day Saturday, and Sunday. They had arranged for Martin and Ceska Cavender, from the Archbishops' Springboard initiative, to do the weekend.

On the Friday of the Holy Spirit weekend, Kathy and I had attended the funeral of a friend who was an Anglo-Catholic priest, Father Rodney Collins. He was a lovely man who had had a stroke, which prevented him from carrying out his priestly duties.

There were three Catholic priests performing the service and it was wonderful. All his colleagues were there. It was just so beautiful and warm. At the end, as the coffin was taken out, a cantor started singing behind us. It was like a rites-of-passage song. It made me cry. The service had a great impression on me.

On that Saturday morning I had arranged to go out and do some archery—a hobby of mine—with some friends after the talk. But after Martin's talk, I couldn't go. I was feeling terribly confused. I went up to him with tears in my eyes and said, "Look, I really need to know if there is a God, because I am getting into such a state. What do I do? How do I find out?"

He was very kind. He said, "It looks like you are in trouble, friend!" He was smiling away because I think he knew that I was right on the edge and just about to go over. Then he ran an impromptu workshop in the afternoon on the gifts of the Spirit. I found that very interesting because it was all very new to me.

Then in the evening it was "How Can I Invite the Holy Spirit into My Life?" We got to the stage where you confess your sins, say you're sorry and ask the Holy Spirit to come. I went through the words and I didn't feel anything. I was quite disappointed. I thought about it all the way home—mulling things

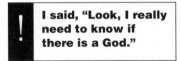

I said, "Look, I really need to know if there is a God."

over in my life. You don't get to be 44 years of age without accruing some baggage. I got home and went to bed.

As I was lying there, I said to myself, "Well, if I am not going to be a Christian, at least I am going to do something about my life." I thought of everything that I wanted to change. I made myself a promise that I would do something about it.

At 5:15 A.M. I woke up and I just brought all those things back into my mind and found myself praying. I said I was sorry to God. I brought everything that I could think of, all that baggage, into my mind. I apologized, hesitated, and then asked Jesus to come into my life. At that moment, I just felt this huge heat coming out from the center of my chest, just radiating out. Massive. Absolutely massive. At the same time I felt this enormous certainty. I was just chuckling and crying. Mainly chuckling, but with an odd tear. I had been very arrogant and self-centered. I have always been a very self-centered person and still am, but I'm not as bad as I was before. It was like there was this wall up and God has knocked all the bricks out from the bottom of the wall and they came tumbling down.

At 5:15 A.M. on Pentecost Sunday morning, age 44, after 24 years as a professing agnostic, teetering between an agnostic and an atheist, sometimes actively arguing against the existence of God, I invited Jesus into my life and He came.

On Wednesday after the Alpha weekend, I told my story to the whole Alpha group.

Kathy was a group leader on the next Alpha course and I was her assistant. Two people in our group became Christians. I don't think people think it is cool to be a Christian police officer. It comes down to individuals. I constantly find that I am visibly a Christian. If I say something and don't do it then other people may suffer. It is not easy, as I still have my obligations as a police officer. I am two positions removed from the officers on the streets, so very rarely do I get involved in active incidents on the street. Some of my colleagues have joined the organization as Christians and have been tested.

We have a Christian group at work. We commit the general problems of policing into prayers. We challenge ourselves. It hasn't all been smooth sailing. I have had two instances where I have gone my own way, back to the old selfish bit. It is one thing apologizing to God, but it is worse still when it affects other people. Martin said to me, "God will give you the opportunity, if you want it, to address an issue from your past. He will make it possible to do that."

He did that to me and it caused me exceptional pain. My faith has increased tremendously. I am more certain in my faith now than I ever was. Also, I have been praying for specific people and my prayers have been answered. I know that they have been answered. It makes me feel a bit frightened and very humble. It could not be mere coincidence.

My wife and I are closer and I am at peace with myself. This is not a hobby, it is a way of life. We have been tested in our relationship. We have been through the fire and have emerged from it very much stronger.

As a Christian, I am a better police officer, without a doubt. My colleagues are pretty frank and they would tell me if I wasn't. I think they find me more relaxed. I don't get as annoyed as I did. I don't take things quite as seriously as I did. I still rush around a bit. I think I am a more even and calmer person. I have an inner assuredness. People I work with have said, "You have changed. You really have changed."

Steve Diddams has recently retired from the police force after 27 years. He and his wife Kathy are now members of the ministry team in their local church and are planning to study for theology degrees at King's College, London. He said, "Since Jesus has become the focus within our marriage, Kathy and I have experienced a peace and joy that neither of us thought possible. My values have changed quite dramatically and I look forward with great anticipation to when God, through His Holy Spirit, is going to take us."

"She looked me straight in the eye and said, 'I'm a Christian,' and turned on her heel."

The story of Simon Downham

Simon Downham, a curate at Holy Trinity Brompton, describes how he rebelled against his Christian upbringing before experiencing an unexpected return to the faith of his family.

I am the son of a clergyman. To be brought up by wonderful Christian parents was a great privilege. Indeed I knew nothing else until the age of 13. I thought all people prayed to Jesus Christ and I remember distinctly at the age of five asking Christ to be my Savior. Then I went to public school and my faith began to drift. I didn't intellectually discount or consciously reject the truth claims of Christianity. I just ceased to see it as relevant. Other things crowded in.

If I'm honest, I was chiefly influenced by the peer group pressure to be "one of the boys." I found that I was good at sports and good at work, and gradually through my late teens there was no relevance or enjoyment left in Christianity. I remember Nicky Gumbel speaking of his experiences when singing that great hymn *Jerusalem* in school chapel. When they came to the words "And did those feet in ancient times walk upon England's pastures green?" everybody knew the answer. No, Jesus' feet didn't walk on England's pastures green. Two thousand years ago, 2,000 miles away, perhaps they did. But it certainly wasn't relevant now.

Anyway, time marched on. I had a year off after school traveling around the United States and eventually ended up studying law at King's College in London. It was there—now totally free of the "restraints," as I saw them, of a Christian lifestyle—that I began to experiment with all those things that I thought everybody else seemed to be experimenting with. In a pseudo-sort of way I began to be involved in radical politics, but I suspect that I was only faking it. I got involved with recreational drugs. I learned more about women and the success of an evening out was measured by how many bottles one had had to drink.

By the time I went to law school I was a dedicated follower of fashion. Whatever the latest intellectual fashion, the latest social fashion, the latest recreational fashion, you'd always find me there working very hard to enjoy myself.

At law school we were required to sit in the same seats in class throughout the entire year and it just so happened that there was this girl sitting four rows in front of me who to my eyes at least, was extraordinarily attractive. Not only was she beautiful, but she was into radical politics, radical music, and radical dress.

At a class party a few weeks after the beginning of the first term at law school I made my first move on this young lady. In those days the technical term was "sharking in."

The only thing I was intent upon was impressing her on how great I was in every area. For some reason the conversation turned to Christianity and I laughed in a sneering manner when she asked if I was a Christian. I gave her my 20 standard reasons why it was pointless being a Christian, at which point she looked me straight in the eye and said, "I'm a Christian," turned on her heel and disappeared into the night. It was one of those situations when I wanted the ground to open up and swallow me.

> **The only thing I was intent upon was impressing her on how great I was in every area.**

Anyway, as was my standard policy, I then avoided her, but strange things began to happen. With the benefit of hindsight I would probably say it was the Spirit of God drawing me back into a relationship with Him. Anyway, I began to feel a profound dissatisfaction, which was compounded by the fact that I thought I had every objective reason to be happy. I had a job lined up with one of the top city law firms. I had a good group of friends. Law school was boring but at least the work was easy and, notwithstanding the most recent episode, I seemed to be popular enough with the fairer sex.

It's difficult to describe how I felt but it's as if I was always trying to achieve something in the hope that it would bring me peace and fulfillment but then, when I had achieved it, finding that it didn't.

There was a gap in my life—something missing, something empty.

It was about the time of the first Ethiopian crisis and the media was deluged with pictures of starving children and I remember being painfully aware of a profound sense of disorientation. It's a bit like the feeling you get when you go into a hall of mirrors at a carnival. Everything in the world seemed out of place somehow—wrong, distorted. Perhaps you know that feeling, when you're surrounded by lots of people and conversation flows but still you feel almost as if you're totally alone.

It was a very odd time and along with those feelings I kept remembering, almost despite myself, the basic teachings I'd learned at Sunday chool, and in my home, about the person of Jesus Christ.

This went on for about four or five weeks and I remembered these words of Jesus Christ—"I am the way, the truth, and the life." Worst of all, I resented having these trite verses coming into my mind. I thought, *I've got to talk to someone about this.*

The only person I thought I could talk to was this girl but that involved pride because I had to pluck up courage to go and speak to her. Anyway I did and, to make a long story short, we talked a lot about Christianity. By the end of a few days of discussion I had four reasons, not 20, why not to be a Christian. Most of these reasons focused on what I thought I would have to give up if I was going to be a proper Christian. I think at heart I had come to see Christianity as a series of don'ts—"Don't do this, don't do that."

We decided to go for a walk around Hyde Park, which was next door to the law school at Lancaster Gate, and as we were walking I had this sense of God saying to me, "Here's a set of weighing scales. In one pan of the scales I am going to put all the riches that I can give you—all the peace and joy and fullness of life—and in the other pan I am going to put your four reasons why not to be a Christian." I saw that what He had to give far outweighed my paltry reasons for rejecting God. I think the girl walking with me sensed that something profound had happened. She said to me, "Would you like to pray?" to which my instinctive reaction was, "No, of course not. What is there to pray about?"

I went home that evening and I knew from all the teaching I had received, all the stuff I'd received in my home, that the one thing I needed to do was to ask God to forgive me and to give my life to Jesus. It took me about an hour to get around to doing it but eventually I knelt down and prayed. The thing that struck me most was that I felt absolutely nothing. And it was as if in that moment God said to me, "I want you to tell your father what you have just done."

Well, it was bad enough going back to speak to this girl about Christianity but to have to admit to my father that he'd been right all along was sheer agony. After a wait of about another hour, I picked up the phone and I remember blurting into the phone as Dad answered it, "Dad, it's Simon. I've become a Christian."

I remember him saying, "Simon, is that you?"

As you can imagine, this was quite an emotional moment and I was weeping and I said, "Yes, Dad, I've asked the Lord Jesus Christ into my life."

I remember that Dad was in a meeting in his study and I heard the people in the meeting clapping. And then my Dad came back on the phone and said, "I'm in a meeting but I'll call you back later.

That's wonderful news!"

During the rest of that evening, my mother called—as did various members of the church at home—to welcome me into the family of God. But the extraordinary thing was that, when I put the phone down after that call, I was flooded with such a profound sense of peace, such a deep sense of joy. I didn't know whether to laugh or cry. It was as if I'd rediscovered an earthly father but something far more profound had happened in obedience to my heavenly Father. I'd discovered this presence. I'd discovered this forgiveness, I'd discovered this acceptance. And I was overwhelmed by the truth that I was a child of God.

Over the next few weeks I devoured the Scriptures. I was in love with Jesus Christ and my heart was changed. I remember going into law school the next day and the same girl in front of me turned around and saw me and smiled—and, much to my annoyance, said, "You've prayed a prayer to Jesus, haven't you?"

Simon Downham worked as a lawyer for six years before training for ordination. He is now married to Anna, whom he met at Holy Trinity Brompton, and they have a young daughter, Ellen.

> *"Even if I go through the deepest darkness,*
> *I will not be afraid, LORD, for you are with me."*
> *Psalm 23:4*

4

"We went to intensive care and stood at Marie's bedside. She was lying there, dying . . ."

The story of Joan Wilson

During the last ten years, Joan Wilson has lived through the tragic deaths of two children and her husband. Her husband Gordon—a beacon for reconciliation in Ireland—died in 1995. In March 1997, she spoke movingly at a Women's Breakfast meeting at St. Paul's, Onslow Square [sister church to HTB] about her faith.

I married Gordon Wilson in 1955. He had a drapery store in the middle of Enniskillen. I was a primary school teacher and taught in the local school.

In 1956 our first child, Peter, was born and that was a great delight. In 1958, sadly, our second child died prematurely—living just a few hours after his birth. That was our first sorrow in the family. We grieved and it took a long time to get over that loss.

Happily, in 1960, our first daughter, Julie Anne, was born and that brought us great pleasure.

Seven years later Marie, our youngest daughter, was born. She was a very bright little girl, very sunny and smiley—and greatly spoiled by her mother, father, bigger brother, and little sister.

She grew up normally, going to the local grammar school, which was just across the road from our home and entered into all the sporting activities she could do. She joined the choir. She played the violin.

She was very loving and caring. She loved cooking in the kitchen and telling me how to do things and how to present plates with plenty of color on them. I was corrected and, at times, Mother could do nothing right! But I didn't mind.

She reached her senior year deciding that she would like to go into nursing. She had completed her Duke of Edinburgh Gold Award and received the award from the Duke of Edinburgh at St. James' Palace, London. She applied to the Royal Victoria Hospital in Belfast for training. She was accepted and after doing quite well in her entrance exams, set off in September, 1985 for the Royal Victoria Hospital.

In November 1987, she came home for the weekend, having completed a training period in the Royal Hospital for Sick Children. She had loved that particular time and came home for two or three days rest before going to the Royal Maternity on Monday, November 9, to train there.

She was very excited about it because she said, "I am going to observe childbirth and that will be very wonderful." So our minds were concentrating on her going off to Belfast on Monday, November 9.

But Sunday, November 8 loomed and it was Veterans Day. Her father always went to the war memorial in Enniskillen to remember and honor the dead of two World Wars. The night before he said to Marie, "Are you going to join me at the war memorial tomorrow morning?" and she said, "Yes, I will go with you, Daddy."

I could never go because I was playing the church organ and I had to go to our Methodist church and be there to receive part of the parade from the war memorial.

On the morning of November 8 they set off. She waved goodbye to me and I remember it was a damp morning and I said to her, "Marie, have you got your umbrella?!" She said, "Of course, Mom, don't fuss! Bye!"

She went off in the car with her father for the four-minute drive down to the parking lot. They parked the car. They walked to the war memorial and took up their position behind the old wall of an unused school.

Within seconds of taking up her position amid the other people, an IRA bomb exploded behind the wall, bringing the wall, the stones and the rubble down on all of the people beneath.

I was at home preparing to go to church. I heard a crack and I thought, *Is that a car door closing? No, it is too hard.*

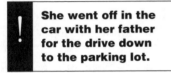

She went off in the car with her father for the drive down to the parking lot.

I thought, *Is it a bomb?* The front door of our house opened and my son Peter came in. He said, "Mom, a bomb has gone off downtown and I think it is at the war memorial."

I said, "But your father and Marie are there."

He said, "I know. What shall we do?"

He and I drove downtown, but we didn't get very far because the area was sealed off and we had to turn and go around another way. I said, "Peter, we will go home again because knowing your father he will call if they are all right."

Peter said, "That is all very well, Mom, but they may not be able to get to a phone." But we did go home and, of course, the phone was not ringing. So he said, "Let's try the church."

At the church, little girls from the Girl's Brigade were coming up the street disheveled and crying and so white. People were in a state of disbelief.

Our minister came to me and he said, "Are you prepared to play? How do you feel? Can you face the organ?" I said, "Well, I am better doing something."

He said, "I have sent your daughter Julie Anne and a social worker to the hospital and they will hopefully send back messengers with some news."

I went in to the organ. We played the first hymn. We had prayer. We played the next hymn and I just realized that I wasn't going to be able to go on. My attitude was, "Let me out of here!"

At that instant a public official came right over to me at the organ and he said, "Mrs. Wilson, will you come with me. Gordon is in the hospital with a broken arm." Peter was waiting in his car for me. I said, "Peter, your dad is in hospital. Where is Marie?"

He said, "I don't know, Mom."

I said, "What do you mean you don't know? Marie set off with Gordon. She must be with him."

He said, "We don't understand anything at the moment . . ." It was a completely new situation—and a terrifying one.

We went to the local hospital. I charged in through the door. People were all around. The place was teeming with helpers. I saw my neighbor and she was crying. I said, "What is wrong Norma?"

She said, "I have lost my two children. They were at the war memorial. I don't know where they are."

I said, "I am looking for Gordon." Then I saw Julie Anne sitting with Gordon. He was in a chair and his shoulder had been dislocated. He was bleeding. He was disheveled and he was just sitting saying, "Joan, where is Marie?"

I said, "I don't know, Gordon. What on earth has happened?"

He said, "The wall fell, but for goodness sake find Marie. Ask people."

I asked so many people and they were all searching. I just could not take in what was happening. I turned to the music master from Marie's grammar school and he just looked at me and said, "The Mullans are dead." That was the local chemist and his wife.

Then somebody else said, "Johnny Megaw is dead."

I just could not conceive that a morning that had started so normally in a quiet little town had plummeted into chaos.

A few hours passed and we searched for Marie. The social worker from our church searched every part of the hospital. People went through the town knocking on doors, asking about her, but no one knew anything.

I had lost a child. If one loses a child at the beach, it is dreadful, and here was I, a child missing. We didn't know where she was or in what condition.

When the social worker had exhausted every part of the hospital looking for Marie, he thought of the operating room. He contacted someone there and that someone (I don't know who it was) gave him a necklace, a bracelet, and a ring. And he thought, *Those could be Marie Wilson's.*

He found Julie Anne and said, "Are these Marie's? Was she wearing a pink frock and blue tights?" And Julie Anne said, "Yes."

He said, "She is in surgery."

Julie Anne came along the corridor and said to me, "Marie has been found. She is in the operating room." A little lady said to me, "She is in the operating room with superficial wounds." And my hopes soared.

But not for very long because an anesthetist came to us and said, "I want the Wilson family together." The only way the Wilson family could be brought together was around Gordon's bed, because by now he had his shoulder set and he sitting up in a bed, still wondering about Marie.

The anesthetist drew the curtains around the bed and said, "Marie is in surgery, but I have to tell you that she is very ill. She has a broken pelvis. She has brain damage. She is hemorrhaging. We have given her 24 pints of blood and she is losing as much as they are giving."

My legs failed. I just could not take it in. Gordon said to him, "Sir, you are telling us our daughter is dying?"

He said, "I am telling you we are fighting for her life and we are doing our very best. We will keep you posted." And they did.

Later, a doctor arrived with the Sister, whom I knew very well. She said, "Joan, bring Peter and Julie Anne up to intensive care now because Marie is there."

Gordon was left downstairs because he wasn't allowed to move for a few minutes. I walked along that corridor and I said, "Please God be in this dreadful situation. I have no help but Thee. Give me strength and Thy will be done." I was so helpless. We were all useless, but we knew that God was there and He was.

We went up to intensive care and another sister met me and said, "Mrs. Wilson, Marie is very weak and her heart is barely beating."

She led Julie Anne, Peter, and myself to Marie's bedside. She was dying. She was lying there, almost lifeless, with scratches on her face. Her eyelids flickered when I spoke and I shall never forget that scene. Shortly after our time in the room she passed on and I just looked at her and kissed her and held her. Julie Anne said to me, "Mom, it is better this way."

I walked out of the room and then back into the room. I walked out and in, back and forth, until Sister took my arm very gently and said, "Mrs. Wilson, you have a very hard duty now. You have got to tell your husband Marie has passed away."

I don't remember going down in the elevator. I just remember arriving at Gordon's bedside and him sitting forward and saying to me, "How is she?" and I said, "She is dead."

He said, "Oh my God, is our child dead?"

Our minister came and just took us in his arms. Nurses came.

Helpers came. Neighbors came who had been sitting and helping all day, who had been searching. Suddenly we were supported by people. We steadied ourselves and then we had to set off for home.

Tom Magowan, our minister, wheeled Gordon in a wheelchair out to the car. Peter drove us. I remember Gordon saying, "The next few days are going to be difficult. We are going to a home without Marie, but we have got to muster all the dignity and love and courage that we can. May God help us."

We went home on that dull November evening and got out of the car and into the dark house and no Marie. We lit the house and it began to fill with people and the phone started ringing and we staggered around.

At about nine o'clock in the evening a young man from the BBC, Charlie Warmington, arrived. I had taught him at school some years before. With him he had a young man, Mike Gaston. Charlie said to us, "May I talk to Gordon?"

I said, "Well, he is very weak and in great pain."

But, Gordon had a room cleared and he went into the room with the two men. Mike simply said to him, "Gordon, tell me your story of this morning."

These are the words Gordon said to him, "We positioned ourselves against the wall and within seconds of doing so an IRA bomb exploded behind the wall. The wall collapsed and Marie and I were thrown forward . . . and stones and dust in and around and over us and under us. I remember thinking, "I am not hurt." Then I was aware of a pain in my right shoulder.

"I shouted to Marie was she all right, and she said, 'Yes.' And she found my hand. And I said, 'Is that your hand, Marie?' and she said, 'Yes.' I kept saying, 'Are you all right?' and she said, 'Yes.' But she was screaming in between. Three or four times I asked her and she always said, 'Yes'—she was all right.

"When I asked her the fifth time, she said, 'Daddy, I love you very

85

much.' Those were the last words she spoke to me. She kept holding my hand and I kept shouting, 'Marie are you all right?'

"Somebody pulled me out of the rubble and I said, 'I am all right, but for goodness sake my daughter is in there and she is not very well.'

"The hospital was magnificent, truly impressive, but we have lost a daughter and we shall miss her."

At that stage Mike said to Gordon, "What do you think of the men who planted the bomb?"

And he said, "I bear no ill will. I bear no grudge. Dirty sort of talk is not going to bring her back to life. She was a great little girl. She loved her profession. She was a pet and now she is dead. She is in heaven, and we will meet again. Don't ask me please for a purpose. I don't have a purpose. I don't have an answer. But I know that there has to be a plan. If I didn't think that, I would commit suicide. It is part of a greater plan and God is good. And we shall meet again."

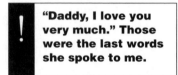

"Daddy, I love you very much." Those were the last words she spoke to me.

That went out on the evening news. Next day it went out on radio and television. It seemed to go all over the world and we had media people on our doorstep.

Those were unforgettable days. We had to face a funeral. By now 11 people were dead and almost 50 hurt and wounded—some very seriously.

One, Ronnie Hill, a headmaster of the local school, was very seriously injured. Ronnie is still lying in bed in a coma after all this time and Noreen his wife is ministering to him day and night. I commend today Noreen Hill's courage. She is wonderful and she is testifying to God's grace and strength in helping her minister to her husband.

The day of Marie's funeral arrived and we had a thanksgiving service in our Methodist church. We were determined that the funeral service would have a note of triumph, a note of thanksgiving. So it had. Our minister preached so well on the text that "nothing can separate us from the love of God" from Romans 8. "Neither life nor death, nor principalities nor powers, nor famine or nakedness, nor height or depth, (nor an IRA bomb, he added) can separate us from the love of Christ."

That gave me great courage. So we laid Marie to rest.

The next day we had to go to the funeral of two of my choir members, Bertha and Wesley Armstrong. That was very sad. The next day we went to the funeral of the Mullans.

And so in that week the town buried its dead and tried to come to terms with a new and different way of living, trying to get through our grief. It wasn't easy, and it took a long time of praying and crying. People were wonderful. We were aware of a great wall of prayer. Thousands of letters came flooding in and we tried to read them. We were so thankful for all this.

Then one day I just wasn't progressing greatly. It was about three days after the funeral. I lifted my Bible and I thought, *How can You help me Lord? I am so down.* In my morning reading I came across 1 Peter 4:12 and 13. These words just spoke to me: "Dear friends, do not be surprised at the painful trial you are suffering as though something strange were happening to you, but rejoice that you participate in the sufferings of Christ so that you may be overjoyed when his glory is revealed."

It certainly spoke to me, but I didn't understand it. I thought, *Well, just today I haven't very much to rejoice about.*

Our minister visited that afternoon and he asked us how we were and talked about different things. He just happened to say, "I don't know what I am going to preach about on Sunday morning."

I suddenly thought of my verse—I call it my verse now. I said to Tom, "I read a verse this morning." And I told him about it. "Would that help?" He said, "It will. I am going right home to write a sermon." And he did. That helped me.

A remarkable thing happened around a month later. I was having a very bad day, crying and just really down. It was a wet day and it matched my spirits. I wandered into Marie's empty bedroom and I was very sorry for myself. I looked at books on her bed that had been sent to us. I had just left them there saying, "I am not able to read those. I can't concentrate. Perhaps some day when I am a bit better I will read them."

But that morning a title caught my eye *Be Still My Soul.* I lifted the book and I turned the page and saw *Be Still My Soul* by Elizabeth Urch and from the author herself signed, "With deepest sympathy from Elizabeth Urch."

I began reading the book. Elizabeth was a primary school teacher who had trained, as I had, at Stranmillis Training College, Belfast. She had married an Elim minister and gone to live in Scotland. They had three children. He was ministering in Scotland to a very thriving congregation and he collapsed one evening preaching.

He had a brain tumor that turned out to be malignant. They operated. He recovered but he knew he wasn't going to live. He prayed that he would be able to preach and thank his congregation for all the praying and caring for him while he was in the hospital.

But he was disturbed because many people had come in to him and asked, "Reverend Urch, why do you have to suffer? Why are you going through all this? Why does God ask you to suffer?" So Elizabeth, in her book, has written out the sermon he preached to his congregation on the text 1 Peter 4:12-13.

I couldn't believe it! Here was this beautiful sermon from a suffering servant saying that just because we are Christians, it doesn't mean that we are going to be exempt from suffering or trials or tribulations.

All the prophets and martyrs suffered and our Lord suffered

more than any of us will ever suffer. He said, "Why not us? We must leave ourselves open to suffering because God is with us in our suffering and because, from the Cross came the beautiful and glorious resurrection. The victory over evil."

I was just so thrilled to read that and I thought, *I must write to Elizabeth.* And I did. She wrote back and we met in Edinburgh. She is a delightful person, living in Pitlochry. She spent some time with me last summer in Enniskillen. We pray for each other and keep contact by phone and letter.

So, that was one of the victories out of the bomb. I can tell you very briefly about two other things.

During that week Mr. Roy McMurty, who was High Commissioner for Canada, was in London and during the weekend of the bomb he was in Belfast with Tom King, who was then Secretary of State. They came to Enniskillen the next day.

Roy McMurty was so upset over what was happening in the province that he set up a program [*called the Marie Wilson Voyage for Hope*] where three Catholics from Enniskillen and three Protestants would go to Toronto, Canada, each summer and live with a Canadian family and go to a camp called Moorlands Camp where there are disturbed children. Our Irish children would work with Canadians helping with them.

This program has been going for nine years and each year I meet the six people who are going to Canada, give them a copy of the Marie book, and encourage them. It is delightful to see them return again, I always meet them in October and they tell me their stories.

Another program, called the Spirit of Enniskillen Scholarships, was organized by Dr. Brian Mawhinney, who was at that time Minister of Education in Belfast. He came to our home in Enniskillen and said, "I am going to try and bring some good out of this."

Gordon said, "Sir, I would like you to do something among young people."

Dr. Mawhinney managed to get enough money from the government to send 30 Catholics and 30 Protestants each year to different parts of the world—to Latvia, France, and Germany where they could share experiences with other young people.

They come back very enriched indeed and we hope that perhaps they will do their bit to making the province a better place.

Those were some of the good things that happened.

Of course, we were in for a lot of criticism because Gordon was accused of forgiving the bombers. We had some very bad hate mail. I wasn't shown all of them. It wasn't an easy ride by any means. But still we plowed on and tried to sow the seeds of love and kindness.

Then came a phone call to Gordon one day from a lady in London who worked in HarperCollins book publishers. She asked Gordon if he would like to write his story.

He said, "Certainly not!" She said, "Perhaps you would like to think about it?" He told me about her request and we decided he was not up to writing a book.

Six months later she phoned him again and he said, "Well, maybe."

She came over to Enniskillen and they met in the shop and she suggested that perhaps she would introduce him to Alf McCreary, who would help with the story. Alf McCreary lived in Belfast and had written a lot about all the troubles. One day Gordon agreed to meet Alf McCreary. He liked Alf and was very impressed with him. He set about writing the Marie book. Alf is very gentle, very quiet, a lovely Christian. God sent him to us and so the Marie book came into being and was launched.

The only reason we wrote that book was that we thought it might help other people. We hoped that God would use it and we prayed that He would. I have had some feedback over the years and I believe that the story has helped other people.

When the Marie book was launched, Gordon went all over the

country telling the story. It took a lot out of him, but it was therapeutic as well as everything else.

Then in the spring of 1993, we were having lunch one day when the telephone rang and it was a call from the then Irish Prime Minister, Albert Reynolds, asking Gordon to join the Irish Senate. Now that was a bombshell in the middle of lunch!

I don't think either of us finished lunch because there was a lot of discussion and soul-searching and phoning and "Oh, I'll ask my good friend so-and-so." We prayed and finally he decided he would accept and go to the Irish Senate.

A very good friend of mine said, "You will be in for a lot of criticism." And we were. "But," she said, "Gordon's presence in the Irish Senate will always be a reminder of the atrocities that can happen in the north of the island."

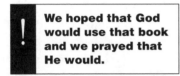

We hoped that God would use that book and we prayed that He would.

He went to the Senate. He received a great welcome. He had been at boarding school in Dublin for seven years and was thrilled with the welcome he was given.

He met Gerry Adams there and spoke to him privately. He counteracted anything he heard about the North that he thought wasn't right. He wasn't afraid to speak out. He was very direct and very honest and had great courage and always concentrated on the facts. He didn't want half-truths; he had to have the facts. He had a very enriching time in the Senate.

After Gordon went to the Senate we were devastated to hear about the bomb at Warrington and the two little boys killed. I phoned Dublin that morning and I said to Gordon, "You must go to Warrington."

He said, "I am going," and he went. He shared with the Parry family and the other family and we sent our sympathies. From Warrington, Gordon was sent back to Dublin with a little teddy bear for President Mary Robinson and he was asked to present it to her. He phoned her secretary at her residence and the secretary said, "Oh yes, she will be very glad to give you coffee at eleven o'clock." They were great friends because President Mary had invited him to Dublin Castle for her inauguration.

Time went on and things were going well. I was glad to see Gordon recovering. By now he had retired from the business and Peter was carrying on.

On the evening of December 7, 1994, I had come in from my teaching. I was preparing to make some raisin cakes for my granddaughters who were coming to supper and that was their favorite bun, and Granny always provided it. A phone call came from my daughter-in-law to say, "Granny, Peter has had an accident. He collided with a truck and it is not very good."

I rushed to their home, the same feelings coming over me as on the day of the bomb. Is he killed? Is he going to be in a wheelchair? Is he brain-damaged?

When I reached the house, I saw my two little granddaughters lying on the sofa crying their hearts out. My daughter-in-law was standing beside a policeman and I said, "Ingrid, is Peter dead?" And she said, "Yes."

Here we were back to square one again and three children gone. Gordon was in Dublin and I ran to the phone and dialed the numbers for Dublin. He came on the phone with a very normal voice and I gave him the news. I said, "Please come home as quickly as you can."

A member of the government drove him halfway and someone else drove his car and people from Enniskillen met him and brought him home. Here we were planning another funeral. I felt, "Well, of course, God is with us again." I didn't dare ask why. I was just numbed and I thought, *My role is to care for my daughter-in-law now and my little granddaughters.*

So we got through another funeral. Half the government from Dublin came to that funeral. It was a lovely service of thanksgiving, but we were lonely and are still lonely and we miss Peter dreadfully.

But at that service we had the fine hymn "Thine Be The Glory, Risen Conquering Son, Endless is the Victory, Thou O'er Death Hast Won."

Our Northern people thought that the people from the South were so warm. And the Southern people thought the Northerners had given them such a welcome. So even in the midst of sadness there was a mingling and a sharing of love and gladness.

The Secretary of the Forum in Dublin—because Gordon was a member of it by now—Wally Kirwan was there. Just a week later, he went off on vacation with his 50-year-old wife. She had a brain hemorrhage and died.

He brought her remains back to Dublin and said to Judge Catherine McGuinness, "I want the hymn 'Thine Be The Glory, Risen Conquering Son' at my wife's funeral." He was a Catholic. That hymn was not in their hymn book, but Judge Catherine McGuinness found it in her hymn book and had sheets copied for the service. They sang that triumphant hymn at Mrs. Kirwan's funeral. We were very touched by that.

On June 27, 1995, during a very hot summer, I had to go to Galway with the school choir. This had been planned for about six months and I set off with the school choir on Monday morning.

On Tuesday morning I phoned my husband. He was in great shape and raring to go to Belfast that afternoon as 60 young people were going out on Spirit of Enniskillen scholarships. He always went, each year, and took me with him to say goodbye to them and wish them well. He was supposed to attend a party in the afternoon at Belfast Castle.

My daughter drove down from Moira that morning to take him

up to Belfast. When she arrived at the house, the doors were open, the windows were open and everything was very still. She called, "Daddy?" But there was no reply. She went around the yard and thought, *Perhaps he is with some of the neighbors.*

But she went upstairs to find him on his bed—dead but very peaceful.

I received the news in Galway at lunchtime. I had just finished accompanying the choir in the *Music of the Night*, Andrew Lloyd Webber's piece. I had just played the last chord when a colleague came over and said to me, "Joan, I have some very bad news for you."

And I said, "Oh?"

He said, "Gordon's had a heart attack and he is dead."

Again, I was taken to a little office and I was trying to come to terms with the shock. The Garda [*the Irish police*] took me out to Galway University where I packed my bag and they said, "We will drive you home as far as you want us to go." In the end, they took me as far as Charlestown and there my daughter and a neighbor and a friend from the church met me.

As I was driven along the road I thought, *Oh, now another funeral.* I knew immediately the hymns that Gordon would want: "Love Divine All Loves Excelling," "Jesu Lover of My Soul," "Thine Be the Glory."

At first I thought, *Peter will help us.* Then I suddenly thought, *No, you don't have Peter. Julie Anne and I are responsible now.* Julie Anne is left, my only child now and thank God for her. I prayed that God would give us the strength to get through. And He did.

The funeral was triumphant and very beautiful. It was wonderful to think that God was again with us. I knew I would have to face loneliness, but by now I knew that God was with me and that His strength and grace would bring us through.

Gordon's message to everybody was from Jesus: love God and love your neighbor. It is a very difficult command. He also went on to say, "Your neighbor is your terrorist neighbor." And people found that impossible to understand, but that is God's command. Gordon said, "Love is the bottom line."

What could I do when we laid him to rest but go on loving and giving the message? There are no answers to these troubles. I set about helping Alf McCreary once again to write Gordon's biography. That was heart-rending and took so much out of me. I couldn't believe it, but I felt it had to be done. It was a memorial to him and perhaps will help others.

I can only end with this message: that in our suffering, in the face of our loss, in our pain and despair, all we can and ought do is to place ourselves in God's care and commend ourselves to Him, remembering His words on the cross, "Father, into thy hands I commend my spirit."

The New England poet John Greenleaf Whittier says it all when he says:

> *I know not where his islands lift*
> *Their fronded palms in air*
> *I only know I cannot drift*
> *Beyond his love and care.*

Joan Wilson continues to live in Enniskillen. She remains a committed member of her local Methodist church, where she plays the organ. She says, "My grandchildren give me great joy. I need God's strength and grace day by day. I thank Him for all that is past and trust Him for all that's to come."

"The man who finds me finds life"
Proverbs 8:35a

5

"With my father's interest in the occult, it seemed almost like a natural thing to be involved in palmistry and tarot. I never felt it was bad at the time. I always did it to help people."

The story of Iain and Fatimah Murray

Iain and Fatimah Murray had no interest in Christianity when Fatimah's sister first mentioned the Alpha course. Apart from running their business, Fatimah was a practicing Tarot card reader and Iain was a Freemason.

Fatimah's story:

I was brought up in Singapore and am the second youngest of 10 children. My father and mother were very strict Muslims. My father was also a great believer in education, however, and the best education in Singapore was at mission schools and convents. He sent most of us to these schools and, not surprisingly, three or four of my brothers and sisters were converted at a very young age to Christianity. By the time I went to school, my father did not allow his children into the religious studies classes because he had seen the effect

97

on some of my older brothers and sisters. After they became Christians, he wouldn't have anything to do with them. He wouldn't talk to them at all. As a result, I hardly came into contact with Christianity at all in my youth, except for hearing about this man Jesus from time to time on the school playground.

I had been born with a hole in my heart—a congenital heart defect—and couldn't do the things that other children did. I couldn't learn to swim or play volleyball or do any of the sports. As soon as I came home from school, I had to lie down. Everybody else was rushing around playing but I had to lie down because of my heart. I remember once, when I was about eight or nine, I heard my parents discussing what my life would be like in the future (in those days there was no open-heart surgery). They were saying that it would be very sad for me because I wouldn't be able to have any children or get married or do any of the normal things that people do.

One day, and I can remember this quite clearly, I said to this man "Jesus," "My friends in the playground tell me that You are a God of some kind. If You are, then make me better."

I was very aware of God as such, but didn't think much about it. My father was very involved in all sorts of spiritism—as are many people in the Far East. He was very much into the occult. My father died when I was 13 and my mother wasn't as strict as he was. Therefore my adolescent years were much more relaxed than they might otherwise have been. Around that time, I made one of my regular visits to the hospital for tests and they told me that my hole in the heart had gone. I could lead a perfectly normal life. But I didn't really think of the prayer I had said. I never really thought of God at all.

When I was 21, I met a man, fell in love, and married him. He came from a nominally Christian family and it was the expected thing for their son to marry in church. I also thought it would be very glamorous to have a church wedding. To do that I had to be baptized and confirmed. I had no understanding of what baptism meant, or of who Jesus is.

My husband was a banker and we traveled a lot all over the world. We lived a very materialistic lifestyle, with a home in Britain where I used to spend quite a lot of time. Whenever there were problems in my marriage, one of the things that I would do was to spend hundreds if not thousands of dollars on shopping trips and feel satisfied for three minutes before going back to feeling totally miserable.

I took a correspondence course in astrology with the Faculty of Astrological Studies in London. With my father's interest in the occult, it seemed almost like a natural thing to be involved in palmistry and tarot, etc. I was very heavily into astrology, tarot cards, the occult. I never felt it was bad at the time. I always did it to help people—to make their lives easier. I never charged for doing it or anything like that.

My husband and I had three beautiful children but, after about 12 years, we divorced. I think it was utter selfishness on both our parts. You can imagine the heartache it caused when we split up.

After my divorce I came to live in England because my children were at boarding school here. I had met Iain Murray at some fancy banking dinner somewhere in the wilds of Borneo and we had became very good friends. He worked in a general trading company in the Far East and traveled a lot. He didn't have a home in England but we met up when he visited.

> **Whenever there were problems in my marriage, I would spend hundreds if not thousands of pounds on shopping trips and feel satisfied for three minutes.**

Not long after my divorce, we decided to marry. We were married in a Methodist church in London and decided to settle in England. By that time I was in the fashion business, buying and selling clothes designed and manufactured in Hong Kong. I bring them in here and sell the dresses.

I wasn't looking for anything much. The children were quite happy, we were happily married and business was going well. We were expanding and, on the whole, life was not unpleasant. I have an elder sister Carol who had become a Christian at the Mission School when we were young and now went to Holy Trinity Brompton. She had been trying to persuade me, certainly in the latter part of 1993, to go on an Alpha course. I was living near Warminster, Wiltshire, and she was living in London. At that time, we were spending a lot of time working in London, which is why she thought I could come to an Alpha course at HTB. I said to her, "Look, let me get to the top of my profession and then I will think about God and Christianity. Right now, I really haven't got the time."

By the end of 1993, I realized I was visiting London three or four times a week and I had never once stopped to have a cup of tea with any of my four sisters who lived in London. My New Year's resolution for 1994 was that I was going to do something about that.

Then on January 2, Carol called me and said, "Look, you must come on this Alpha course." I said, "Look, I am terribly busy. I haven't got the time." Then I thought, *You silly wimp! You have been saying that you are going to spend time with your sisters and the first time they ask you to do something you make an excuse.*

I said, "I don't really want to come to an Alpha course, but if you and I want to get together for anything after January 12, I will gladly come and see you."

"Oh, hang on a minute," she said, "our Alpha course starts on January 12."

I agreed to come. It was a hassle, because I wasn't spending that day in London, but having made that commitment, I thought that I couldn't let her down. I was working in Wiltshire that day and had arranged   to   meet

Carol at her house at 5:30 P.M. I missed my train and I said to her, "I am terribly sorry," rather gleefully. I explained I had missed the 3:30 P.M. train (due to arrive at 5:00 P.M.) and that the next one would be too late for me to meet her. She said, "That's all right. Come straight to the church. Take the next train. Alpha doesn't start until seven."

> I said to her, "Look, let me get to the top of my profession and then I will think about God and Christianity.

So I got into this taxi at Paddington and traipsed down to Holy Trinity Brompton wondering what I had let myself in for. I walked into this room where everybody looked surprisingly normal. I didn't see any weirdos or coots! For all that, I actually found Nicky's talk on "Who Is Jesus?" rather boring. Then we broke up into small groups and I don't think I was very nice to them.

I said, "If you Christians think you are the only ones who will go to heaven, I will stay in hell with all the Muslims and Buddhists who are probably quite good people as well." There was another woman who was very involved with the New Age so, together, we gave everybody an extremely hard time.

They didn't say a word. They didn't argue with me or anything. All they said was, "Why don't you come back next week?" I had already made the decision that I wasn't going to come back. So I said, "Thanks, but no thanks. I work on Wednesday evenings and I am not coming back."

They said, "Don't worry if you miss a few. We have tapes."

I said, "No, really, thank you, you have been very nice. I enjoyed my dinner, but I am not coming back."

When I left the church I apologized heartily to my sister because I was sure that I had been such an embarrassment to her. She was very nice about it. She said, "Look, you said you would come and it doesn't matter if you don't want to come anymore. Don't worry about it." I stayed with her that night because it was a bit late to go back to Wiltshire.

> **I walked into this room where everybody looked surprisingly normal. I didn't see any weirdos or coots!**

The next morning, everyone had gone off to work and I was left in the drawing room waiting for Iain to come and pick me up. I wasn't really thinking about what had happened the night before, but I saw an Alpha manual sitting on a table. I was leafing lazily through it when suddenly I had a vision of a Man standing in front of me who said, "After all I have done for you all of your life, why do you reject Me?" Then He took me back to the time when I was five years old and had the congenital heart defect. He showed me that it was Him who had made me better. He also took me back to when I was going through my divorce. My husband wasn't being very kind. I had no money to carry on living (I wasn't working at that time). Suddenly there was a windfall. I had some land in Singapore that had been sold. I had completely forgotten about it. This money just came the mail. It seemed as though there was somebody there looking after me.

He showed me all the times in my life when He was there for me. I just sat there and I wept and I wept and I wept. I thought I was having a nervous breakdown. How can I describe it? I saw intense, extraordinary love. It is hard to imagine. The thing is that people always say to me now: "How can you be so sure?"

I can say, "Yes, I have met Jesus Christ personally." I could never deny Him now, no matter what happens in my life. I can never deny that fact of Him standing in front of me and loving me in that way. I didn't really want Iain to know what had happened, because I was sure that somebody was going to commit me somewhere if I told him what had happened. I kept it to myself for two days.

On Saturday night we went home and I was cooking. I said to Iain, "I think I have met Jesus Christ." He asked me to describe it. He said, "I suppose you are going to say that suddenly there was a bright light and this Man was standing there in front of you, and there were little angels playing harps and trumpets." I had to say that it was all of that and much, much more. It was impossible to describe.

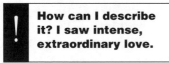

How can I describe it? I saw intense, extraordinary love.

He screamed with laughter and told me to have a good night's rest and not worry about it. The next morning was Sunday and Iain had to go off on business and was away for the whole day. I woke up that morning with a burning desire to read the Bible. It was totally overwhelming. I had never opened a Bible before that day.

The trouble was I couldn't find one. I remembered that my son had one in his school trunk up in the attic. I remembered that because he had gone to a Christian school and they demanded that we buy him one. I rushed into the attic and found this much desecrated Bible and sat down and tore through Matthew, Mark and most of Luke. Iain came back at ten o'clock and I hadn't brushed my teeth, I hadn't made the bed, I hadn't done anything. I just sat in my nightgown in our television room reading the Bible.

I had a million questions for him—which he couldn't answer, of course. He just thought that I had gone completely mad. I called my sister and said, "I have got to come on Alpha. I must find out more." I told her about my vision.

Then I started going to Alpha every Wednesday. Iain was wondering what I was doing. We were running a business where we had to do seminars on a Wednesday night. I just said, "I am so sorry, I can't do the seminars on Wednesday night anymore. I have to go to Alpha."

I spent most of my time on Alpha crying—during the talks, during the worship. Every time the name Jesus was mentioned, I would just weep. I suppose that was my conversion. On my second night on Alpha, some people in my group, including my sister, prayed for me and I found myself saying, "Lord, I give my life to You. I just love You so much." I was sitting weeping and saying, "You can have everything. I will do everything for You." In the group were all these wonderful people. They could not have been more wonderful. It was an extraordinary time in my life.

> **Every time the name Jesus was mentioned, I would just weep.**

Within about three days of becoming a Christian, I felt I had to throw my tarot cards away. By this stage, Iain had started reading the Bible too (we were very close and he wanted to read what I was reading). I said to him, "I have got to throw all my astrological books away."

He said, "You can't do that. They are worth more than $3,000. At least sell them to the second-hand shop."

I said, "I can't do that. I have got to throw them away. I have got to burn them, in fact."

"Well, couldn't we give them to a library?" he said.

I said, "No, we can't do that."

"Why?"

I said, "I don't know why. I just know that I have to get rid of them." I had to wait about two weeks before he got around to recognizing that I was talking sense.

Everyone in my group was praying with me that Iain would come to at least one of the Alpha talks. But our business gave seminars on Wednesday evenings and he had to be there to take them. Then one

Wednesday night, everything that he was doing got canceled at the last minute and he came. I was there already because I had taken the earlier train, but he came in his car. I didn't know he was coming. When he walked in, I was flabbergasted but everybody else just sat there and looked as if they expected their prayers to be answered. Then Iain came with me on the Holy Spirit weekend, which was being led by Jeremy Jennings. He wasn't going to let me go on my own with all those "strange people." By that time he was into the Bible and I think he was already well on the way to becoming a Christian.

God gave me the gift of tongues on Saturday and I was so excited that I didn't stay for any of the skits on Saturday night. I just ran up to my room, sat on my bed and started praying in tongues—all evening. There were just waves of love, which was the most extraordinary experience.

Then I went to bed. When I woke up in the morning, I noticed there was something different about me. For many years, I'd had a damaged shoulder and I'd been unable to lift my arm up. Yet when I woke up in the morning my shoulder was completely loose and well.

I said to Iain, "Did you do something with me last night?"

He said, "Well, I had this buzzing in my hands. Some time afterward, Jeremy had said how God sometimes gives a sense of tingling in the fingers when he is giving a gift of healing. I wasn't going to tell anybody about it—not even you. But I thought, 'Lord, I am going to put my hand on Fatimah's back. If it really was You giving a gift of healing, please heal her shoulder.' I then prayed for your shoulder."

After that our life was like a roller-coaster. Extraordinary things happened. We just gave our lives to God totally. Within about two months, we had the rug pulled out from under our feet financially. We had to give up a lot of things and sell the Mercedes and that sort of thing.

Our lives changed in that I felt I needed to pray and read the

Bible for at least an hour or two a day. That was really important to me. Iain was finding the same thing too. Sometime after that, we started running an Alpha course in our own area of Wiltshire. We met some of the local clergy and ministers and invited the Catholic church, the Anglican church, and the Baptist church to send people. They came and other courses grew from that.

After that, the Roman Catholic priest asked us to run an Alpha course for him, which we duly did. Since then, we have helped other churches get Alpha courses up and running.

> "In the Far East, it was part of the
> normal routine to be a freemason."

Iain's story:

My father was a Church of Scotland agnostic and my mother was a fairly laid-back Catholic. My father didn't go to church himself but rather supported the children being taken to the Catholic church.

When I was at school in Edinburgh, I went to Catholic mass on Sunday mornings and the Protestant school chapel in the evenings. The denominational infighting seemed so hypocritical, I didn't want anything to do with any of them. I opted out of church life altogether at the age of about 15.

I was in the Army for 15 years and then worked for a business in the Far East based in Sarawak and Brunei.

By that time I was married, but my wife and I had lots of fights and she ended up running off with an Australian. The marriage lasted a year and a half.

It was a relief to me, as it had been a difficult situation and I couldn't see any way out of it. I wanted out but I wasn't prepared to start divorce proceedings. She started the ball rolling, so that was that.

While I was in the Far East, I became a freemason. It seemed quite natural out there, part of the normal routine. You played golf, did the bar scene and, if you fit in, you were invited into freemasonry. Being quite a transient part of the world, with a lot of businessmen coming and going, I moved up the freemasonry ladder very quickly. I did in five years probably what would take somebody in England about 15 years.

I went into four degrees of freemasonry and became Master of a Lodge in Brunei. I was invited to seek higher levels in Kuala Lumpur but every time I arranged to go, business or other urgent matters prevented me, so I never got any higher in freemasonry.

I met Fatimah out there and after her divorce we were married in a Methodist chapel in north London. We settled in Wiltshire and I did attend the odd lodge around the area with various friends, but I was officially a member of a Scottish lodge which made it rather inconvenient. I kept in touch, but that was about it.

Fatimah and I had just started our clothing business and had quite a reasonable lifestyle. We had money coming in. Then Fatimah went to the Alpha evening in London with her sister Carol. I did our business seminar in Salisbury that night, which meant she was able to go.

I picked her up from Carol's house and she was fairly tearful. I thought perhaps I had done something wrong. I wasn't really sure what was going on.

The following Sunday I was away all day in London. When I came back, Fatimah was just sitting there still in her bedclothes reading this rather tattered old Bible. She told me all about a "revelation" she had had at Carol's house, where she had met Jesus.

I said, "Yeah, yeah, yeah. I suppose there were trumpets and horns and an angelic choir," and she said, "It was all that and more." I listened very skeptically.

She then started going to Alpha every Wednesday. This was a bit of a strain because I was then doing all the Wednesday evening seminars.

I was saying, "Look, what is this that you are doing? Where are you going? What is it about?" And she said, "Well, read the book" and gave me *Questions of Life*, which I did read.

It was the first chapter, on "Who Is Jesus," with its textual criticism, that appealed to me. I have an engineering degree so I have been taught to apply logic to everything. That was why I had rejected Christianity in the first place. I didn't think the Virgin Birth, the Resurrection, or Creation were logical, but reading that chapter put everything into perspective.

Once I had accepted the Gospel as logical, I had to accept that it was true. I started reading the Bible because of that. From Creation on, it all began to fall into place.

Then one day, I said, "I would like to attend an Alpha evening, but there is no way I can because of these seminars."

Then one Wednesday soon afterward, I had six guests I was due to teach at the evening seminar. One by one all the guests canceled. It was four o'clock and I realized I could get to London for Alpha at seven o'clock. So I drove down there.

> **I have been taught to apply logic to everything. That was why I had rejected Christianity in the first place.**

As I walked in, Fatimah was quite surprised to see me but members of her group said, "Oh, we knew you would be here. We have been praying for you to arrive."

I looked around and I didn't seem to have anything in common with anybody. I thought they were really strange. I thought, *What is this group that Fatimah has gotten involved in?*

I thoroughly enjoyed the talk, which was given by Sandy. I

thought it was first class. From then on I started reading the Bible more earnestly.

A little while later, Fatimah said she was going to Brighton for the Alpha weekend. I said, "You are not going to Brighton with that bunch of coots without me."

She said, "You can't come unless you give up freemasonry." That was a bit of a red rag at the time because one doesn't say that to a freemason. Her group seemed to think freemasonry was wrong too. There was a little bit of cooling as I was quite angry about it.

As I read the Bible in the days after that, I came across these verses in Matthew 6:33: "Don't swear on anything. Let your yes be yes and your no be no. Anything else comes from the evil one." We take an oath on a book in freemasonry. It is called *The Volume of Sacred Law*, which is the Masonic Bible. But I never read it, so I just presumed it was a standard Bible.

Then I read another verse in Corinthians which says, "Don't be yoked with unbelievers." I knew that verse referred to marriage but in freemasonry, of course, you accept all comers as long as they believe in a "supreme being." The verse seemed to say to me that I was associating with unbelievers in what was a spiritual exercise.

Finally I read in Acts 4 about Jesus being the capstone. In one of the freemasonry degrees (relating symbolically to architecture) the capstone is the key feature. It struck me that if Jesus is the capstone and one must follow His teachings, and that He says not to take oaths on books and things, there is a contradiction.

With all this evidence, I felt I had to give it up. Later, some verses of the Epistles, saying that as Christians we are "heirs with Christ in the riches of heaven" and (in 1 John 1) "In God there is no darkness at all," gave me confirmation. A Christian is neither poor, nor in darkness—the symbolic entry into freemasonry.

So, at two o'clock on Friday morning before the Alpha weekend, after Fatimah had gone to bed, I just went out in the middle of the night and burned everything to do with freemasonry that was mine and I wrapped up and mailed anything that was not mine.

I have an incinerator trash can, so I just stuck them in there. It took me awhile because some of them didn't burn too easily. I wanted to do it alone because I didn't want Fatimah to say, "I told you to do that." I wanted it to be my own decision.

Then I wrote letters of resignation to the various lodges that I had belonged to, not in bitterness, because I had actually gained a grounding in Scripture from freemasonry that I hadn't appreciated, but because I just realized that they were on the wrong path.

In my letters, I explained that I had seen the light of following Jesus and I hoped that they would one day follow me on the right path. I wrote to everyone—even the Grand Lodge. I received charming letters in reply, for which I was grateful.

Later that Friday we went to Brighton. I was fascinated by the teaching on the Holy Spirit. I heard that the gifts were free from God, and that we should eagerly desire them.

I particularly wanted healing because my mother was very ill. While they were praying for the gifts, my left hand started tingling. I thought it was pins and needles. It just got more and more painful.

It was absolute agony. I didn't know what to do about it and it kept going all evening. At night after the party I went to bed. Fatimah was already asleep and when I got into bed I put my hand on her shoulder and said a prayer because I didn't know what else to do.

She had had a bad shoulder and she hadn't been able to exercise or lift her arm or anything like that, because she had wrenched it very badly two years previously. So I prayed and went to sleep.

I thought no more about it in the morning. When I got up, I was just going out when Fatimah said, "Did you do something to my arm last night?" Her shoulder was totally healed. She was moving it everywhere. It was really extraordinary.

I am now a completely committed Christian. I don't know how to put it into words. Jesus is just the total focus of our lives—absolute. I am always falling off God's path, but I get convicted so fast when I do anything wrong. I just love the Lord and have such joy knowing He's guiding me.

The only thing that I can recommend to freemasons is that they focus on the fact that Jesus is the capstone and look very closely at all Jesus' teachings and then make their own judgment. They will find that, although the path at the start is very similar, it is actually a separate path.

It is so subtle. Freemasonry preaches charity, good works, brotherly love, all sorts of things. You don't discuss religion, politics or business. So at the level that people come in—and the normal three degrees of freemasonry—it seems to be on the surface, very right.

The problem is that it is man-made and when you start getting into the higher levels, the amount of internal politics that goes on is just as bad as any other man-made organization.

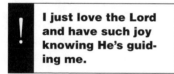

I just love the Lord and have such joy knowing He's guiding me.

Also, there is a definite spiritual dimension to it. There is a power generated by freemasons meeting together in what is a form of ritual prayer. There is no question about it—you can feel the power.

Once, when I was master of a lodge, we had a meeting at home and everybody was gathered in my house. Fatimah sat in another room and she said that she could feel the power of the presence. The higher you get in that game, the more the path starts diverging and you get onto the wrong track.

I am incredibly thankful that by God's grace I have come to know Jesus. Our lives have changed wonderfully and immeasurably.

Iain and Fatimah Murray continue to live in Wiltshire where they help several churches organize Alpha courses.

"It is like I have been scooped up by a helicopter . . . and hauled me back to dry land when I was in total despair."

The story of Karen Lanaghan

With her own apartment, comfortable lifestyle, and assured self-confidence, most people thought successful lawyer Karen Lanaghan was completely happy with her lot. What they didn't realize was that she was becoming increasingly desperate that her life had no purpose. Here she tells how her search led to a remarkable series of "coincidences" and the realization that Jesus Christ is alive today.

I was christened as a baby and my parents vaguely believed, but we didn't go to church as a family. When I was about eight or nine my cousins started attending Sunday school and so I went along with them until I was about 16 and then I stopped going to church completely. I went to Brunel University, near Uxbridge, and the few Christians that I came across, I didn't like.

I am a person who works out what I want to do, learns the game rules, sets my mind to it, and just does it.

When I was in my third year at the university I decided I wanted to become a lawyer, mainly because my best friend was a lawyer. So after getting my degree, I went to law school. Then I made it through the Bar exam and had to do internships for two years. Then I was a qualified lawyer.

But I started to feel that there was something missing. I didn't know what it was. Everybody kept telling me I had a perfect life: I had lots of friends, a great job in London, a car, and I went on lots of vacations. But something was gnawing away inside me. First of all I changed jobs, but I still felt something eating my inside.

Then I thought, *OK, it must be insecurity because I haven't bought an*

> **But I started to feel that there was something missing. I didn't know what it was.**

apartment. So I bought an apartment. I looked at four and bought the fifth one. It was all done within about six weeks, but I kept thinking, *There has got to be more to life than this.* Then I thought that I must just be bored with my friends, so I stayed at home for six months and decorated the apartment. But I still felt that something was missing. I started to think, *What is the point of getting out of bed in the morning? What is the point of going to work if I am only going to go again tomorrow?*

Next I thought, *What I need is a boyfriend, a good relationship.* So, I called up all my friends and said, "Hey, I am back on the scene." So, for six months I hit the party scene and got back to my usual sociable self. I got into some tricky situations with men, and the parties and attention didn't stop me feeling empty inside.

Then I thought, *I am too self-absorbed. I am not doing anything for anybody.* So, on New Year's Day 1996, I decided to do some charity work. I stayed in on a Tuesday evening, sat in my hallway and read through the Yellow Pages, marking charities that I thought I could help. But no one wanted me! They only wanted my money.

Then I thought, *Maybe, just maybe, I ought to go to church.* It was a last resort. I had tried everything else. So I went to three churches in the Fulham area one Sunday evening at around 6:00 P.M. and they were all closed. Then my central heating broke down. The logical

> **Then I thought, "Maybe, just maybe, I ought to go to church." It was a last resort.**

thing would have been to call the gas and electric company, but for some reason this was the absolute final straw for me. I just fell to pieces.

The first night I stayed at

home and cried and cried and cried. Then I got up and went to work the next day. Then I came home and cried some more. The gas and electric company was coming the next day, but they didn't come—they were late. I absolutely fell to pieces. I called up a friend and said, "I have got to come over and have a bath."

She didn't know what on earth was the matter.

I turned up at her house at nine o'clock in the morning. I was crying. She had a baby and her baby started to cry. She was also expecting another one and was feeling emotional anyway, so she started crying. I was crying, the baby was crying, she was crying—it was chaos!

I had a bubble bath, returned home and the utilities truck came. Then I pulled myself together and got back to work. After that, my friend invited me to go with her on a Christian weekend. I said, "No, no, no. God is not for me. I know it has nothing to do with me."

I said I would baby-sit for her on Friday evening so that she and her husband could go out for dinner. When they came back they said, "We really think that you should come on this weekend. You are obviously tired out. You just need a break." Then I felt: why not? They are friends. They played it very low key, explaining that it was a church class reunion but I didn't have to go to any masses or classes if I didn't want to.

It was a Roman Catholic church Easter weekend at a school called Stoneyhurst. I met two priests there and I had chats with them. Then one priest said to me, "How long have you been a Catholic?"

I said, "Actually I am not."

He said, "What are you doing here?"

I said, "It's a coincidence. It is a long story." And so I told him the story about the central heating.

He said, "Did you ever consider that it might not be a coincidence and that God might have actually wanted you to come?"

I said, "Oh, don't be ridiculous."

The phrase kept cropping up over the weekend: maybe it is not a coincidence. That was one thing that stuck in my mind. Then I started talking to a novice priest and he said to me that I obviously didn't believe that God loved me. I had never really heard anything about God loving anyone to be honest. I thought He was just an angry, judgmental God who told you off when you sinned. The idea that God might love me was very strange. I came away from the weekend with two thoughts: first, maybe it was not a coincidence and, second, to allow for the possibility that God might love and be interested in me.

> **I had never really heard anything about God loving anyone to be honest.**

After that, I went along to a traditional, formal church about three times. I didn't learn anything. I got nothing out of the worship. I didn't understand what I was doing there. Consequently I thought, *Karen, you have had a bit of a brainstorm and a few people were a bit kind to you. Just get on with life and stop whining.*

The next Sunday I thought I would drive over to the church where that novice priest who had spoken to me was based. It was in Clapham. But the church was closed when I got there. I was driving back toward South Kensington when I came to a roadblock on the Fulham Road. For some reason, the road was closed off, so I had to detour onto a one-way system. I ended up at a T-junction with a church in front of me. It was about 6:50 P.M. and there were a few people milling about outside. I remember thinking, "What are those people doing milling about outside the church?"

I was wearing glasses and leaned forward to see what kind of church it was. I couldn't quite read the board. I lifted my hand to push my glasses up my nose and the chap on the other side of the road thought I had waved him over!

He came strolling over and said, "Hi!" and I said, "Hi!" He said, "Are you looking for a service?"

I said, "Well, actually, I was. But the church I went to was closed."

He said, "Well, why don't you catch the end of this one, because we are only halfway through?"

I thought, *Catch the end of this? That is a bit trendy isn't it?* So I said, "What kind of church are you? Are you Church of England, Catholic, Baptist?"

He said, "We are the parish church of St. Paul's Onslow Square and we are the sister church to Holy Trinity Brompton."

I said, "Oh no! You're the happy clappy lot! I am not coming in there!"

He said, "I suppose we could be described as happy-clappy, but we don't think that there is anything wrong with enjoying worshiping God. I would love to talk to you but, unfortunately, I can't." He patted his bottom and he had his drumsticks in his back pocket. He was the drummer from the worship band. I couldn't believe it!

He looked really disappointed when I said I was not going in. I felt bad then for being so nasty. I drove around to the edge of the church and there was this massive parking space and I thought, *Oh dear, maybe it is not a coincidence that the other church was closed. Maybe it is not a coincidence that the road was blocked. Maybe it is not a coincidence that this guy came over to talk to me. Maybe it is not a coincidence that there is a parking space. So maybe I had better just go in.*

So I went in and stood at the back. There was a talk going on and within a very short space of time I was crying. I had never experienced anything like it. It was as if the speaker was talking directly to me, as though he knew me. At the end of the service they had a song. It was so moving. I think it was something like *My Jesus, My Savior* and I was just struck by it.

The next Sunday I came back to the church. This time I got there at about 6:20 P.M. I wanted to sing but I just cried all the way through. It was very moving. John Peters was talking that week and he said something about Alpha. At the end of the service I marched up to the front and said, "Well, what kind of a church is this anyway?"

Then I launched into all sorts of questions about baptism, at which point he said why didn't I come on Alpha?

I thought, *There is no way that I am going on any ten-week course with a bunch of Christians.* I thought John was a bit casual, anyway, because he wasn't wearing the garb vicars normally wear. Then he asked me whether I thought I was a Christian. I said I had never murdered anyone and hadn't done any stealing, so I thought I probably was. Then he asked whether I had a living relationship with Jesus. I thought he was a complete wacko because so far as I was concerned Jesus was dead. Nobody had told me that He was alive.

He told me Alpha was on Wednesday evenings. The following Wednesday, I was going on vacation to the Canary Islands, so I said to John that I couldn't come to the first week anyway because I was going on vacation. He said, "Well, come the next week."

But I said, "I can't because I am coming home that day."

"Well, come on the third week then."

I said, "I can't come on week three of a ten-week course. Surely not."

After that I suddenly found I had this desire to read the Bible. I went home and started reading the Bible. I took it on vacation with me. On the last day of my vacation, I called my sister, who is a year younger than me and lives in Coventry. We are best friends and are very, very close. It was 9:30 P.M. British time and she wasn't in. Normally I would never say to her husband, "Where is she?" but I said to him, "Look, it is 9:30 P.M. on a Tuesday evening. Where is she?"

He said, (I could feel him look around his own hallway and drop his voice to a whisper) "She's gone to church. She's started a course and I think it is called Alpha."

I just couldn't believe it. I almost dropped the phone. I thought, "This is no coincidence! There is no way this could be a coincidence. I went to a church that runs an Alpha course and my sister, who lives 100 miles away, who doesn't know that I have been to church, who herself has not been to church for 15 years—apart from her wedding and the christening of her two children—is starting a course."

It was unbelievable, so I thought perhaps I had better give this course a shot after all. I came back to England, went to church on Sunday evening and then, on the next Wednesday, I went to Alpha week three, which was the story of why Jesus died.

Basically, it blew my mind. I just sat there and cried all the way through the talk, ran into the ladies' room and cried buckets. I pulled myself together, came back out, and got a cup of coffee. I knocked the coffee over, cried again. It was a complete fiasco.

John had told a story to illustrate why Jesus had died and how it was in order to save people. It was the story of a bus driver who lives on a mountain and every day he drove around and around the mountainside, picking up all the children, putting them on the bus and taking them to school. He had been doing it for 20 years and had gotten to know the families really well. It was a routine thing and he knew the road well.

One day he was driving down and he realized that his brakes had failed. What was he going to do? He had a split second to decide how he was going to save all the children on the bus. He remembered that there was a flat field at the end of the hill and if he could drive through the gate, he might be able to control the bus, bring it to a halt, and save the children.

So he decided that was what he was going to do. Then, at the very last moment, just as he was about to steer towards the gate, he saw a child playing right in front of the gate. He had to decide between killing that child outright or swerving and risking all the other people on the bus.

He drove straight through, killing the child outright, but all the other children were saved. All the parents came running down the hill and everyone was rejoicing because all the children had been saved.

The bus driver himself was completely desolate because the child he had killed was his own son.

For me that was the most shocking story I had ever heard in my life. I was absolutely stunned. I just cried and cried for about 20 minutes. Then we got into our small groups. By this time I had gotten back into my cynical lawyer mode.

I said to everyone, "It's all right for the kids on the bus. They were probably brought up in Christian families. But what about me? Where is the bus-stop? How do you get on the bus?" I was really furious that all these special children knew how to get on the bus and would be collected.

One of the girls in our group was a Chinese lady called Pansy who is really lovely. She said to me very simply, "Karen, it is a request bus stop. All you have to do is ask. You just put your arm out, the bus stops and you get on. It is as simple as that." I laughed out loud. I wasn't laughing at her. I was laughing at the sheer simplicity of it. After that, I got a real passion to read the Bible again. I was up on Thursday night until 5:20 A.M. speed-reading in true lawyer style—just couldn't put it down. I started at Genesis and got to the end of Leviticus. I read all the Gospels, Acts, Corinthians, and got to about Philippians.

The next Sunday I went to both the morning and evening service. I had a hunger to come back and hear more. I had agreed to have Sunday lunch with some friends who live halfway up the highway, so I had to come speeding down

> ! **I wasn't laughing at her. I was laughing at the sheer simplicity of it.**

there to get to church on time. I was actually late for the service.

As I opened the church door, I thought I was going to be knocked flat. I felt a physical presence I had never felt before in my life. I had to grab hold of both doors to stay upright. I couldn't believe it. They were singing a very quiet song and I thought, *It is true! It is true what people have been saying that whenever two people, even only two people, come together in Jesus' name, His Spirit is in their midst.*

I couldn't believe it. I felt the Spirit of God and it was incredible. But I still didn't believe that God was interested in me and I still wasn't a Christian. I didn't say anything to anyone because I didn't know anybody.

After the service, I went to the front and hoped someone would come up and pray for me to prove to me that God knew me personally. But no one prayed for me that day.

So I left, got into the car and drove home. I still felt the need to read the Bible. It was 9:30 P.M. and I sat at the kitchen table and started to read. Then I felt such a presence. It was like those Vietnam films when you see a helicopter and people have to duck their heads down to run out of the helicopter. I felt just like that. I felt like I had to get down.

In my own kitchen, I just threw myself on the floor. I am talking decked out facedown on the floor. I was wearing a pair of clean trousers and my kitchen floor was dirty. And there I lay for two hours. I prayed to God like I had never prayed in my whole life. When I got off the floor it was 11:40 P.M. and I was a Christian. And that was that.

I can't really tell you what I said. I know that it was from deep within me. I knew two things that I prayed for. I understood from Alpha that it was important to repent and ask for forgiveness of sins. I had done two bad things in my life that I had been carrying around with me for years.

I left a friend at a vacation camp and ran away to meet a boy. Leaving her was bad and meeting up with him was bad because he actually had a girlfriend. I had felt guilty about that every single day of my life for about five years. I prayed for forgiveness for those things. I asked that if I could be forgiven, then I wouldn't ever do anything like that again. And I would give my life to God.

That is all I remember praying. I am sure I wasn't praying about that for over two hours. The rest I don't know. But it was true prayer. That was May 19, 1996.

I woke up the next day and I couldn't eat. For over two years I had been constantly sad and empty inside and I had been giving Oscar-winning performances—looking perfectly happy and cheerful to the outside world.

Now I felt bigger—as if I couldn't get my clothes on. I felt almost like I couldn't breathe, that my lungs at the back couldn't get air into them. I just felt taller. I felt like a physical weight had been lifted from me. I have never felt so cheerful. I was a different person—as simple as that.

I couldn't eat for three days. I couldn't get this thing out of my mind.

I came to work and my secretary and I had the usual routine: "Morning Karen." "Morning Hilary." "How are you?" "Fine, fine." "Have a nice weekend?" "Yes, thanks. Did you?" "Yes, thanks." Into the office.

I could hardly say to her, "I threw myself facedown on the kitchen floor and gave my life to God." I didn't even know what I was doing, but I knew that I had done it. It was unbelievable.

What happened after that was that I started slowly to tell my friends and at first, they thought I had gone mad. They are starting to realize now that it is not a phase. They know that I have changed.

As the summer wore on, my life changed dramatically and I kept going to church. I felt a real peace that I hadn't felt before. I started to have a sense of purpose, which is what I had been lacking. A sense of direction. A sense of belonging. A sense of understanding where I fit into the scheme of things. A sense of hope.

There are so many other things I could tell you, the amount of coincidences that have happened since I first got that phrase in my head: "Maybe it is not a coincidence . . ."

I became a helper on the next Alpha. I found it fantastic. I have such a hunger. I have absorbed so much. I have nearly read the whole Bible. I just have Joel, Amos, and Revelation to go.

Before, I felt that life was futile. Now I have a real happiness and fulfillment that I have never known before. I can't just say, "I've got a bit of inner peace." I am a totally transformed person—absolutely and utterly.

I know I am turning into a walking cliché but Jesus is literally the Savior of my life. I know everybody has heard that before, but it is like I have been scooped up by a helicopter that has grabbed me at the last minute and hauled me back to dry land when I was in total despair.

Karen Lanaghan has temporarily left the legal profession to manage a ski resort in the French Alps. She said, "I thank the members of my women's prayer group at home for their steadfast love and support."

> "He and his family were filled with joy,
> because they now believed in God."
> *Acts 16:34*

6

"I couldn't love my son."

The story of Val Sillavan

On August 18, 1996, Val Sillavan and her husband David celebrated their 40th wedding anniversary by renewing their vows during the Sunday morning service at Holy Trinity Brompton. This was an unusual event, but Mrs. Sillavan had written a deeply moving letter to HTB Vicar Sandy Millar earlier in the year asking if it might be possible to do this. This is what she wrote.

David and I were married in HTB in 1956 and had three children. We never went to church or thought about God at all. Our middle child, a boy, gave us great problems, leading to much grief and fights between David and me. At 18, Nicholas set off for Europe. Seven years and much heartache later, God met him in the Tokyo underground in 1984 and he had a "Damascus road" experience, when he was at the bottom of the barrel, as it were. He gave his life to Jesus, joined YWAM [*Youth With A Mission missionary organization*] and is still a missionary in Japan. To us it was just another "phase" of Nicholas's and gave us no comfort at all. My husband and I were at

125

the end of our "road" also at this time and we divorced. Can you imagine Nicholas's confusion and grief? Here he was praying his parents would become Christians and instead—we divorce!

Three years later Nicholas married a lovely half-Japanese Christian girl and at their wedding my husband and I met again and fell in love again, and we and our three children and their spouses ALL went away on the honeymoon together to my daughter's London home! It was a wonderful time. We remarried and lived in total peace and harmony.

In 1990 Nicholas called to say they would like to spend the summer with us. I felt dread as there was always trouble between David and me when Nicholas was around, and I treasured our new-found love and happiness very deeply.

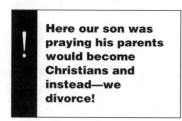

Here our son was praying his parents would become Christians and instead—we divorce!

Telling David that Nicholas was coming, I confessed something I had not even realized before: I didn't love my son. I knew I should— every son deserves the love of a mother. I don't know when it died, but it had, and I felt very sad and very guilty.

When he came I saw a fine man of God, a marvelous husband, father and son, but I thought sadly, *It's all too late. Though I respect and like what I see, I don't love him, and I can't manufacture it.*

He asked me to come and hear him give a sermon. I refused. I hated churches. I found them threatening and sermons bored me. But the Holy Spirit was working, and that night I felt great guilt: "Could I not even do this for my son? What sort of mother was I, not even prepared to hear him talk?" So I went.

I was so intensely moved from the beginning. My son's smile was so sweet—I never saw that smile at home and I realized that here he was with people who loved him, where he could be himself. I saw the many lines around his eyes and I thought, *This is my son. He's only 31 and yet how much he has suffered to become the fine man of God he is now. How little I helped this angry struggling boy to find himself. What a poor mother I was.*

His sermon was wonderful. It was about David and Mephibosheth in Lo Debar [*"Land of No Pasture"*] and I ran out crying. At home David said, "Why are you crying?"

I said, "We love each other so much, you and I. We have forgiven each other everything. Why can't I love Nicholas enough to forgive him? Why can't I love him enough to get over the past?"

Later Nicholas and Ioanna, his wife, both asked me how I felt and I cried a lot and told them how much I'd failed as a mother and how poor Nicholas should have had someone who could have helped him, understood him, and what tremendous guilt I felt.

I also poured out to Ioanna all the pain and bitterness I felt over hundreds of incidents, and for two hours that dear girl listened to my anger and grief about the past. I never told either of them that I didn't love Nicholas.

That night in bed I just wept and wept for the past, all the lost times, the years one cannot recapture, a childhood gone, years of pain and fights between David and me.

Bitter memories devoured me and I felt such anger, such guilt over it all, and grief and remorse overwhelmed me, for when I thought of the Nicholas I now saw, this fine young man, I still felt it had all come too late. Still I could feel no love for him, and I could not feign love.

All I could feel was the anguish and pain he had caused us. I didn't even have photos of him around the house as I felt a real pain in my heart when I looked at them, but I had put up a few before he arrived.

And throughout the night of agony I longed to read the Bible—I was amazed! I wanted to read again the story of David and Mephibosheth, but I didn't know where there was a Bible in the house.

I fell asleep at about 5:00 A.M. and had an amazing dream. I was sitting bowed down on the dry stony desert under a burning sun and I knew I was in Lo Debar —The Land of No Pasture.

I felt as if the weight of the whole world was on my shoulders. So great was the grief, guilt, remorse, and anguish that filled me, I felt totally alone in this desolate place. Then someone held out his hand

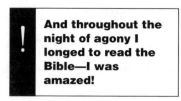

And throughout the night of agony I longed to read the Bible—I was amazed!

to me and I took it. He raised me up and led me out of that wilderness over a beautiful blue river onto lovely green meadows on the other side. The river was lined with trees and I looked up and the leaves were all the tender new green of early summer. The sun was coming through them, dappling the grass, a gentle lovely warmth, not that burning heat of the desert, and as I stood there all the weights fell from my shoulders, all the anger and pain, the aggression and grief, the guilt and remorse and I felt young and happy, light and free, and full of such joy as I looked around in wonder at the beautiful place I was in. Then I woke up.

The sun was pouring into my bedroom and I still felt that same happiness and joy—no more sorrow and guilt, no more anger and regret, just this amazing peace and joy. Then I looked at my bedside clock to see the time and it was 7:30 A.M., but behind the clock was a photo of my son and, as I looked at it, love flooded into my heart and I stared in amazement. Then I leaped out of bed and looked at all the other photos around my room of him and love just kept pouring into my heart for my son. I loved him with the same intensity and sweetness that I loved my daughters and I knew that God had performed a miracle.

He had given me back my son through His Son—and tears just poured down my face. I ran in to Nicholas and said, "Oh Nicholas, I love you so much! Will you read that Bible story to me?" Can you imagine how he felt—my son—with his mother asking him to read the Bible! He was seeing a miracle happen before his very eyes!

Since then I have loved the Lord with all my heart and soul for He has returned to me my husband and my son in such miraculous ways. I know that few people are granted second chances with relationships, and I treasure them deeply.

My youngest daughter and her husband in the U.S.A. came to Christ one year after me. Hallelujah! My husband was very anti-God for three years, then the Lord worked further amazing miracles and he came to the Lord in 1993. Isn't God good?

If you have gotten this far you may be wondering what this has to do with you! Well, God put a thought into my heart last year that I dismissed as being impossible as we are both bad travelers, particularly my husband who goes nowhere if he can help it.

But the thought lay in my heart like a precious dream until Christmas Day, when suddenly it all came together. I suddenly found myself pouring out these words to David: "Darling, years ago you and I stood at the altar of the Holy Trinity, Brompton, to be married. We cared nothing for God and thought only of ourselves. Now we both know the Lord and my greatest desire is to stand together before our Father, on our 40th anniversary—and I feel this is what He wants too—to meet us again in that special and anointed church, now that we know Him and love Him. We have wandered for so many years through the desert, and I feel He is saying the time has now come for us to stand before Him to thank Him and praise Him for all He has done in reconciling us to each other, and to Him, and restoring the years the locusts ate."

My husband agreed at once and I looked to see what day our anniversary falls on. My son immediately felt in his spirit "Of course it will be on a Sunday, for the Lord has ordained this."

And indeed it is. On August 18, 1956, we were married in your lovely church.

Yours sincerely,
Val Sillavan

David and Val Sillavan worship at a non-denominational church in Macclesfield, Cheshire where Val helps with children's work and leads the missionary prayer. Nicholas and Ioanna remain missionaries in Japan.

"After the talk I realized for the first time that Jesus was actually God."

The story of Sharon Morrell

Sharon Morrell was an "agnostic" and her husband Gary an atheist when Sharon attended an Alpha course at her local Roman Catholic church. Her experience led to Gary attending the next course. Now both are Christians and churchgoers. Here Sharon tells her story.

My mother was a Catholic and my father was an atheist. Although it was very strange, he decided to send me to a Church of England school. I didn't really take anything in regard to religion while I was there. Although it was a church school I had never participated in anything in the church.

When I left school, I couldn't actually believe there was something there. I would have called myself agnostic. Apart from school, my only experience with church was going to weddings and funerals. I was married in the church attached to the school only because I like the building. It created beautiful wedding pictures.

My husband Gary was a complete atheist, not an agnostic. His mother was Catholic, his father Church of England. We had two sons, and they were both baptized, just in case there was something there. I had never been baptized, even though I attended a church school. Gary was quite happy for the boys to be baptized.

Although I had never gone to church, one day I was asked by my mother-in-law to cook the Catholic priests' dinner. She had been asked if she herself could do it, but as she is a lousy cook she asked me to do it for her. I believe now that was the beginning of my journey. There were three priests in the presbytery that I cooked for—all very nice people, but that is as far as my regard for them went. They never spoke to me about religion and I greatly respected that.

The secretary at the presbytery, Pauline, mentioned to me that she was starting up an Alpha course shortly and invited me to go. I really thought this type of thing was not for me, and I didn't want to go. But she said, "You'll find it very interesting." I told her that I was a vegetarian, thinking that this would put her off, as she had explained that they start with a meal.

A while later, I got a phone call stating that the course was starting on Tuesday night and a special vegetarian meal had been arranged. I felt that I had been cornered, but I didn't want to hurt her feelings so I told her that I couldn't come because I couldn't drive and therefore couldn't get there.

Pauline said that this was not a problem. She would get someone to pick me up. She urged me to come this once, and if I didn't like it I didn't have to come again.

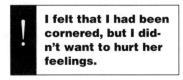

I felt that I had been cornered, but I didn't want to hurt her feelings.

On the first evening I thought, *This is not for me.* But after the talk I realized for the first time that Jesus was actually God. That made sense to me. That was the beginning of the jigsaw coming together.

If I could have gotten out of the second evening I would have but Pauline had organized another lift and another vegetarian meal. I felt that perhaps she was desperate for people to come, so I went again.

It wasn't until the third week, when we were shown a picture of Jesus standing at the door [*a painting by the artist Holman Hunt shown during an Alpha course*] that I felt anything touch me personally. I just couldn't stop thinking about that picture.

I was still against going on the weekend away. I still wasn't convinced that this was for me. However, I had to let Gary believe that I wanted to go, otherwise I was afraid he would tell Pauline very strongly that I didn't want to go and she was wasting her time on me.

So there I was on the weekend away. On the Saturday morning we had a time of prayer. Although I didn't realize it at the time, the prayer was for the Holy Spirit. I imagined the door in the picture I had seen in week three, and I opened it. I felt a tremendous feeling of release. I now know that a healing took place and the only way I can explain it was that I felt very spiritual.

After the weekend Gary became very interested and said that he would like to do the next course. Everybody else couldn't wait for their husbands to do Alpha after them, but I was the exact opposite. I didn't want him to do it. I was very panicky about what he might say.

Gary started the next Alpha course and I spent the whole ten weeks worrying whether or not he was upsetting everyone. When Gary's weekend came up he was sure he was going to get "zapped" by this Holy Spirit. This didn't happen and he was very disappointed; but he still wanted to continue the course.

Afterward, he went on to do a follow-up course to Alpha based on the book *Questions of Life* with Brian and Maureen Devine. This is when things began to happen for him. He had received the Holy Spirit in a completely different way. He started to be very evangelistic to the point where friends would tell him to shut up. But because of him, a lot of our friends have done the Alpha course. I could never have achieved this. I would have been too embarrassed.

He has changed dramatically. He now thinks about his actions continually and about the effect they have on others. He has always been very kind and has always done things for others. The difference is that now he does what he does because he is a Christian and he does it for Jesus. Corny, but true.

The most remarkable thing that I can actually put into words is the effect that Alpha has had on our relationship with one another. Two years ago I really did not believe spirituality existed in the church—certainly not within Christianity—but I was wrong. Two years ago I went to see Father Taylor lunchtime and asked him if he would baptize me. I was received into the Catholic Church last Easter.

Gary and I now pray for one another quite openly and naturally and it is wonderful to be able to share that together.

I am still amazed at how becoming a Christian can change people. Before becoming a Christian I could not tolerate children. My own were easy to love but I now find myself being drawn to other people's children.

Later, in my new faith and enthusiasm, I expected all my Catholic friends to be as open as I had become. This was not to be the case with some of them and I have had to learn to curb my enthusiasm and accept everyone where they are on their journey.

Sharon and Gary Morell remain members of their local church into which their son, William, was received on Easter 1998 after completing an Alpha course.

> "The children have noticed a difference. They just said, 'You have changed. We can see it in your face. That depression seems to have gone from you.' "

The story of Derek Fox

For more than 20 years, mailman Derek Fox delivered mail to the vicarage of Holy Trinity Brompton—but he never went near the church until August 1996. Here he tells how his profound depression when his wife left him has given way to a new happiness and hope in the future.

When I was a child I used to go to Sunday School in the afternoons. We had Bible lessons and used to sing hymns in the hall. My parents never used to go to church. After that, I used to go to weddings and christenings and things like that. My wife and I never went to church. One of the last times I went was in 1977 when my mother died. She died of cancer and was really in pain. I just went to the early morning service and prayed. But that was it.

Then, in 1987, my wife started to go to church quite regularly—to the Sheen Baptist Church. She became a "born-again" Christian in—I think—November 1987 and was fully immersed in water.

She had quite a religious background from her own family. But it never sort of appealed to me at the time. I was busy working. She quite often would say to me, "Why don't you come to the church?" and I would say, "No, no." She always wanted me to go to church but it never appealed to me.

Then on July 30, 1995, she suddenly told me that she wanted to leave me. I am still not quite sure what the full reasons are because she won't talk about it. She just says that she feels we have grown apart and she doesn't love me like she used to. I didn't know what to do, so I just got down on my knees and prayed. I didn't know if I was praying correctly. It was just in desperation. I just prayed and prayed. I became very depressed, so I went to the doctor who gave me anti-depressant tablets. They ended up doing me more harm than good. They took all the water away from my body and I lost 28 pounds in six weeks. I still haven't put it back on. I've gone from 210 pounds to about 182 pounds.

> **Then on July 30, 1995, she suddenly told me that she wanted to leave me.**

When I finally went back to work, I was delivering some letters to the vicarage when Annette [*Annette Millar, wife of Sandy Millar*] came out and said, "Oh, I haven't seen you recently." I said, "Well, I've been ill." And I just felt compelled to tell her what had happened. So I told her that my wife had left me and that she was a Christian.

I will always remember her reply. She said, "God won't like that." Then she said to me, "Do you know God's phone number?" and I said "No," with a little smile.

And she said, "Well, it's Jeremiah 3-3-3." [*The Book of Jeremiah, chapter 33, verse 3, reads, "Call to me and I will answer you and tell you great and unsearchable things you do not know."*] She gave me a Bible and wrote it down and that was that.

The next time I saw her she had left a little package for me. It was Nicky Gumbel's little book *Why Jesus?* and another little book similar to the one that was on the Alpha course [*Questions of Life*]. So I took the package home and opened it up. I read the little one *Why Jesus?* all the way through. I said the prayer suggested at the end of it (saying sorry for everything we have done wrong and asking Jesus Christ into our lives) but it was not a significant moment.

Then, when I turned the book over and looked at the back I just couldn't believe it. I thought, "Now, God, this can't be right!" Because on the back it said the printers were called Kingsway and I live in Kingsway in Sheen. It just seemed more than a coincidence.

After that, I kept bumping into Annette and Sandy. Sandy told me he was very sorry about what had happened and invited me to church, which I accepted.

When I walked into the church for the first time one Sunday morning at eleven o'clock, I couldn't believe it. The place was just sort of alive from the ceilings to the wall. *Is this a church or is it a party?* I thought.

Everybody seemed so friendly and happy and smiling. All the little children and babies were there. It was like a new world. I just couldn't understand it.

It was not a church that I was used to going to, where you go into it and it is all stone and it smells dank and you only see half a dozen people sitting in pews. But, no not this. It was brightly done. It was lovely.

The following Sunday I went again and I was happy. Then I went to the front at the end of the service and had hands laid on me because I felt that I had to ask for help. When I walked out I felt light—as though it had taken a big weight off my mind.

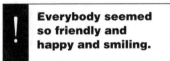

Everybody seemed so friendly and happy and smiling.

I continued going to church on Sunday mornings. Then someone said, "Have you thought of doing an Alpha course?" And I said, "Not really."

They gave me a pamphlet about it. I was thinking, "Yes, I will"—"No, I won't"—"Yes, I will." I didn't know what it consisted of.

Then one day I suddenly got a registered letter for Sandy Millar. I knocked at his door and he answered. I said, "I've got a registered letter for you." He signed it and in the next breath I said, "Can I have a form for the Alpha course?"

He said, "Yes." He searched around and got one. I just filled it out at once and delivered it through his mailbox.

So I started on the Alpha course. I found the first one quite slow, but I thought I would continue because people in the group that I was in said it was good. I just carried on, but it wasn't until the fifth week, which was all about prayer, that suddenly it all seemed to come together for me. It was also the first week that I remembered everybody's name in the group, so that was a good thing as well!

A couple of weeks after that was the weekend away. Again it was, "Yes, I will go"—"No, I won't"—"Yes, I will"—"No, I won't."

I told my group it was a little difficult for me because I only get one in every six Saturdays off in my job. They told me the date and I got out my diary—and it worked out that my Saturday off was that very weekend.

I said to my two children—Julia (22) and Neil (19), "Should I go?" They said "Yeah, you go Dad." I said, "Are you sure you are going to be all right?" They said, "Don't worry about us. You go and enjoy it."

I was a bit reluctant because I was going on my own. It seemed quite a big step. But anyway, I said, "Yes, all right. I'll go." I got someone to take me, because I wasn't sure of the way.

On Saturday, Nicky Gumbel talked about the Holy Spirit. In the afternoon, he asked the Holy Spirit to come. I was thinking to myself, "What's going on?"

He said, "Don't take any notice of the people around you. Then suddenly, as I stood there, I began to feel tingling in my left hand. It was like little electric shocks—similar to when you walk on one of those carpets and touch something and you get a "ding!" But this tingling was all the time.

Then two team leaders laid hands on me and suddenly all these tears started coming out the side of my eyes. Great big teardrops were coming down my cheeks—only out the sides—just pouring down. I felt that it took all the rubbish out of me.

Then suddenly I became all hot and they just sat me down. I was still wiping my eyes. By this time my handkerchief was absolutely soaked. They just said, "Stay there." But it didn't matter because I couldn't get up. I was stuck there anyway.

I felt exhausted. After about 10 or 15 minutes I decided to get up. I felt all light and smiley. I was walking out and I bumped into the couple who drove me down in the car.

The wife asked, "Are you all right?" And I can remember shouting out, "I am now!"

She said, "You look absolutely lovely. Your face is aglow." I said, "I feel great."

I went and got changed and had dinner. The next day we had another meeting and the Holy Spirit was asked to come again. I was just standing there and it came quickly this time. First I had all this tingling in my left hand and up my arm. Then my leg started shaking. They laid hands on me again. I was completely crying this time, sobbing like a child with tears pouring down. I was also boiling hot again. They sat me down and said, "Stay there." I did—well, I couldn't get up again.

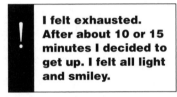

I felt exhausted. After about 10 or 15 minutes I decided to get up. I felt all light and smiley.

When I got up this time it was as though I was a new person. I had forgotten about the past. All I was interested in was the present and the future. I was so happy and joyful and so full of confidence that I felt I wanted to shout it out. All my depression had gone completely away from me.

I felt that it gave me all the joy and love and confidence I needed to get me through the trauma of what had happened with my wife. I did pray afterward, "Thank You, God, for baptizing me with Your Holy Spirit." I can remember saying that and I felt a great relief.

My group leader, Ivor, said he would give me a lift home. In the past, I would have sat in the car looking out the windshield, talking a little —"yes," "no," and so forth—and that would have been it. But Ivor and I must have talked from the time we left till the time we got to London. We never stopped talking to one another. We were just babbling on about everything. When I arrived home, the children asked me, "Did you have a good time?"

I said, "Yes, really great!" And they looked at me all peculiar and said, "Are you all right, Dad? You're different." I said, "Well, I feel sort of different. I feel rejuvenated, happy."

I am definitely a different person than the person I was before my wife left me. I'm a completely changed person. I don't get uptight. Nothing seems to upset me. I seem to sort of turn the other cheek when it comes to something stressful.

When I was in the traffic jam in the car, I used to mumble to myself about how fed up I was. I don't get uptight about that now. I work in an environment with lots of men where everybody is swearing all the time. I used to join in and say all the swear words—sometimes every other word. But I haven't sworn since coming back from the weekend away. It might sound strange but that is absolutely true.

Now I can find other words to take their place. I never used to swear at home because of my wife and my children but now I don't swear at work or at home.

The children have noticed a difference. They just said, "You have changed. We can see it in your face. That depression seems to have gone from you." The depression *has* lifted, but I do sometimes have down days, like over Christmas and New Year's Day.

I've seen Jesus forgive my sins. I was angry at my wife and I was saying that she should be punished, which is the wrong attitude for a Christian to take. If she is going to be punished it is not for me to say so.

I want to find out so much about the Christian faith. I've started reading the Bible. I've read the New Testament and I've now started reading the Old Testament. I've bought a book from the bookstore that gives me a reading in the morning and in the evening each day.

My wife knows I am a Christian but I think she felt, "He's only doing this to get me back." But it wasn't like that at all. It was just that I didn't know where to turn. I just prayed. And it wasn't until I met Annette and Sandy and was compelled to tell them what had happened and they invited me to church.

Now it's got to the point where I find on Mondays I'm looking forward to Sunday when I can go to church. I really look forward to it. With prayer, hopefully, my wife and I can sort this out. The door is always open for her. I'll have her back without a doubt.

She knows that I have changed and that I am a different person.

Derek Fox continues to worship at Holy Trinity Brompton, where he is a member of a home group. He and his wife remain separated, but he says, "I know the Lord has changed my life for the better since becoming a Christian. Through prayer God gives me strength to come out of the kingdom of darkness into the kingdom of light."

7

"I was leaning across the table staring into her eyes when Jacqueline said, 'There are two things that you need to know about me. They will turn you off completely.' "

The story of Gregory and Jacqueline Gottlieb

As Gregory Gottlieb's career in the Army developed, his churchgoing childhood gave way to a life of drink and enjoying time with the opposite sex. Then he spotted a girl at a party to whom he was instantly attracted. It was a meeting that was to have a profound impact on his life.

My father was a churchwarden in our local village church, but apart from my mom, my dad, myself, the vicar, and the other churchwarden, hardly anyone else went. I went there from the age of about six until the time I went to boarding school when I was eight—and then on school vacations after that. I grew up on a farm near Eastbourne in Sussex and at that time felt very close to God. I had some wonderful times just sitting in the fields talking with the animals and with God.

At boarding school I went to chapel, but by the time I was a teenager I lost interest really. By the time I was a teenager I became more interested in doing all the other things that

143

boys do—like playing with computers, listening to music, and staring at the small number of girls that were in my class.

I joined the Army as soon as I left school and they sent me to the university, where I went completely wild. I read psychology at Goldsmith's College, London, and was heavily into alcohol. I also made it my mission to meet as many girls as I could and get to know them as well as I could. I was leading a fairly promiscuous life, which made me quite depressed because none of the relationships were based on anything. It was quite a dark period.

On breaks, I spent most of my time in Berlin with the First Battalion Grenadier Guards. Berlin was a pretty wild city at that time (the early eighties). Everybody lived as if there were no tomorrow.

When I left the university I went back to be retrained by the Army. At that time, I was heavily into the paranormal: telepathy, telekinesis, healing—things like that. I didn't ever get into the darker side of it—the ouija boards—but I was always aware that there were very powerful forces involved. Every once in a while—maybe once a year—I would go to church, but I didn't really see the point. My mother had died and my father had moved and his church involvement had faded. I was working in London doing public service—guarding the Palace, etc.

In 1984, two years after leaving the university, I left England to spend two years working with the Army in a remote part of Australia. I was very lonely there. About a year into my tour there, I met a lovely girl named Sandy who was a flight attendant with an airline. She came to town often and, it being such a small place, we had nothing to do but drink and get to know each other.

Then I was told I was being reassigned back to Northern Ireland a bit early. We decided that rather than lose contact and lose the relationship that we had built up we should get married.

She came to town often and we had nothing to do but drink and get to know each other.

She was a Roman Catholic but didn't like going to church. Nevertheless we were married in a church and had two years in Northern Ireland. Then we came to London where Sandy got into a lot of New Age things. She became a *shiatsu [a Japanese massage therapy practitioner]*. I just didn't feel comfortable with it and we found we were spending more and more time apart and we mutually agreed that the best thing to do was to call it quits. We walked into Wandsworth County Court hand in hand, rang the buzzer and said, "Can you tell us how we get a divorce?" The girl on the other side said, "I wish everybody did it like that." The divorce was finalized in 1989.

Soon I was back to my bad ways of having girlfriend after girlfriend. In January 1994, I went with a girlfriend to a Chinese New Year's party—a fairly lively private party with 300 to 400 people in a club. I was a Major at this stage, with a desk job in the Ministry of Defense. During the party, I looked across the room and my eyes caught the eyes of this quite stunningly beautiful woman. I remember my heart leaping. Despite not having met her, I just knew that she was going to be my wife. I was in the middle of a conversation with somebody I think and I just stopped and stared at her. I thought, *Gosh, I'd better go and introduce myself to her.* She was there with a whole group of friends.

I thought to myself, *There is no way this girl is even going to speak to me, but I must go and talk to her.* So I managed to corner her at one point, in between her dancing with other men and said, "Look, I am terribly sorry, but I am not going to let you leave here until either you have given me your phone number or I have given you mine."

She said something like, "Well, I've been thinking pretty much the same thing about you." You could have knocked me over with a feather! She said, "Here's my number—where's yours?" Her name was Jacqueline. I then went back to my girlfriend and said, "Look, I'm awfully sorry, but I've met this amazing person, whose phone

145

number I've taken."

She was extremely understanding, because she is that sort of girl. She canceled the chauffeur-driven limo she had ordered to take us back to her home and instead dropped me at my apartment. It was all very civilized. Two days later I took Jacqueline to a little restaurant in central London. I made sure the restaurant was less than four minutes walk from my apartment and that we had a nice bottle of wine in the fridge at home, ready for later on.

Halfway through dinner we were getting along famously. I was leaning across the table staring into her eyes when Jacqueline said, "Before we go on there are just two things you need to know about me. They will turn you off completely, so please let me finish my meal."

I thought, *Uh-oh, here we go!* "What are they?"

She said, "The first thing is: I have a five-year-old son." And I said, "Yes?" (Thinking, *Well, that really doesn't matter and it's certainly not going to make any difference to tonight or for the foreseeable future.*)

"And the second thing is," she said, "I am a born-again Christian which means I am celibate."

I remember having to work really hard to keep my smile composed. But I thought to myself, *Well, actually does that matter?*

And for the first time in my life I knew that it really didn't matter at all. I had already reached the point of no return with this woman. We just got on amazingly well. Then our courtship started immediately. What I didn't know and didn't discover for some time was that Jacqueline had effectively been a single parent since her son, Alexander, was ten months old.

She had been a Christian for about two years. Before the Chinese New Year's party, Jacqueline had been upset and Alexander had said to her, "Mommy, I want a new daddy and I am going to pray that Jesus gives me a new daddy now."

When he went to bed he said, "Please, Jesus, will You give me a new daddy?" And apparently in the background Jacqueline was praying, "And please make him tall, dark, and handsome." (He obviously didn't answer the entire prayer).

A couple of days later she met me, but that ties in with something a bit later on. Jacqueline had been married for about three years and then went through an exceptionally painful divorce, after her husband had left her. Jacqueline lived in Northampton and on my first visit there, she took me to her church—a Baptist church just outside Northampton.

> **"And the second thing is," she said, "I am a born-again Christian which means I am celibate."**

It was like nothing I had ever experienced in my entire life. It frightened me. It made the hair rise on the back of my neck. There was lots of shaking of hands, the occasional hug, people putting their hands in the air . . .

The pastor was a very charismatic speaker. Nobody was being somber and Church of England-ish. Instead, the music was modern with guitars and singers with microphones. It was only a small church and it was packed. At the same time, with hindsight, I think one of the things that made me feel uncomfortable was that I felt something there that I hadn't felt for a very, very long time—since my childhood. Anyway I was happy to go along with Jacqueline because I was falling head over heels in love with her.

We went there a few times. We also went to the Kensington Temple, where again I wasn't particularly comfortable. All the while, I respected Jacqueline's celibacy absolutely. We kissed and cuddled a fair bit, but I was quite happy to go along with that. For me, that was unique and it really surprised me.

On Easter Sunday 1994, we happened to be in London. We had heard about HTB and decided to go. We sat a third of the way back, slightly to one side. From the moment the first song started I burst into tears—floods of uncontrollable tears that lasted for the whole service. I am quite an emotional person. When I am on parade and hear really stirring martial music, I have to grit my teeth. But in church, in public, actual tears—NO, not me! It hadn't ever happened in church. I just couldn't stop, however hard I tried. I was thinking, *Oh, God.* That then turned into *Thank You* because obviously something was happening to me that I didn't understand.

When Sandy [*HTB Vicar Sandy Millar*] spoke, I remember listening to what he was saying and thinking that it was the most valuable lesson of my life. I can't remember the subject of his sermon. At the time every word seemed a golden raindrop. Something was happening to me that was very powerful. Afterward I was very embarrassed. My handkerchief was absolutely sopping wet. Jacqueline was grinning from ear to ear and thanking the Lord for coming into my life and that I found a bit annoying. I just thought, *Golly, what is happening to me?*

After that, we never really stopped going to HTB. I never wanted to walk out of the building—I wanted to stay there. Suddenly, I was able to communicate with God in the same way that I could when I was seven years old. It was like a door had been reopened.

We decided to get married at HTB. When I asked about the possibility, I was told that because I lived just outside the parish, I would have to do the Alpha course first. When they explained what it was, we said, "Yes, that sounds great." So we signed up for the summer Alpha course in 1994.

> **I can't remember the subject of his sermon. At the time every word seemed a golden raindrop.**

Alpha was the most extraordinary thing that I have ever been involved with. I said a prayer giving my life to Jesus the first week of Alpha. I just followed the prayer that Nicky suggested. We were in Bruce Streather's group and we met some amazing people there—truly amazing. We have made friends from our Alpha group who will be with us for the rest of our lives. It helped me in so many different ways. To say it changed my life sounds a bit crass—but it did. I just drank in everything I heard.

Gregory Gottlieb recently resigned from the Army and he and his family will shortly be moving to Germany, where he has a new job. Gregory and Jacqueline remain regular churchgoers despite some "very tough" times.

In the next story they describe how their faith helped them through the sickness of their newborn son. Since then, Gregory says, "We have found it hard to balance the needs of a demanding young family with our need for quiet time together and with God. But our commitment to Christ remains absolute."

The story of Daniel Gottlieb

Gregory and Jacqueline Gottlieb tell the story of how their faith has been strengthened following the birth of their twins, one of whom, Daniel, nearly died.

Gregory:

We were married on July 21, 1994, and when we came back from our honeymoon, we went on a sort of second honeymoon with Alexander —to Toronto, Canada, where we had been invited to a wedding. During the summer before we married, Jacqueline had been diagnosed as having a massive cyst on her ovaries that resulted in the doctors being unsure whether she would be able to conceive.

Jacqueline:

I went to the General Practitioner and he referred me to a gynecologist for a hysteroscopy. It was discovered that I had a very large uterine fibroid and, after the hysteroscopy, I was told that I also had quite a large ovarian cyst.

I went on the Alpha weekend and at the end of one of the sessions, somebody came up to me and prayed for me. I told them that I had a problem—that we had only just got married and I really wanted to have a baby, but the doctor had said that I would probably need some help because it was going to be difficult for me to conceive. They just prayed over me. I felt very warm and relaxed. It was a wonderful weekend and I just felt very good. It was a small group, two or three people. They prayed that I would be healed.

The following Monday I had an ultrasound and the doctor couldn't find any trace of the cyst. It had completely disappeared. He kept me there for nearly an hour.

He said, "I can't believe this! Only last Thursday, I felt the cyst and it was there." It was now Monday. I remember leaving the hospital feeling wonderful and saying, "Thank You, Lord!" because I just felt that everything was going to be okay.

Gregory:

Just before we went to Canada, Alexander, who was four, said in his prayers one evening out of the blue, "Dear Jesus, please can I have some brothers and sisters?"

Almost as soon as we got back from Toronto, Jacqueline was very ill and became very depressed. We discovered she was pregnant, which was very exciting, but she remained ill. We simply didn't know what the problem was. We just prayed and hoped it would all work out. When Jacqueline went for her first scan after three months, the nurse looked at the screen and didn't say anything to her. She just said, "Before I say anything I am going to go and get your husband."

> **The cyst had completely disappeared. He kept me there for nearly an hour.**

Jacqueline was really worried about this. I was waiting outside and the nurse—looking absolutely poker-faced—came and said, "Please come in." And I thought, *Uh-oh. Why isn't she smiling?*

I remember sitting down on Jacqueline's left-hand side and holding her hand and the nurse saying, "Well, I can tell you exactly why it is you have been feeling so sick. You are going to have twins." I burst into tears. Now that we knew why Jacqueline was so ill, that eased things a little bit.

When Jacqueline was seven months pregnant, we went to a 7:00 A.M. prayer meeting at HTB. Toward the end of it, Deidre Hurst offered to pray for Jacqueline, me, and our babies. Suddenly, I had a very vivid vision. I saw the Lord Jesus standing with a big smile on His face, holding our two babies, one in each arm. I couldn't see the features of our babies. For me, they were just like glowing little faces. From that moment I knew that we were going to have healthy twins and that they would be all right. It was a very moving experience— but all the more so because Jacqueline later said she had had exactly the same vision at the same time.

Jacqueline:

I also saw Jesus with the two babies. We had made the decision not to have any tests and I did have some concerns, but after that vision I knew that they were going to be fine. We prayed every day for the babies. We read the book *Praying for Your Unborn Child* and Gregory sang the song "Lead Me Lord" to the babies every night.

Gregory:

Some months before, we had moved to the Army married quarters in Kingston. This must have been all part of the Lord's work because it meant that the babies were to be born in Kingston Hospital, which had just opened a new Maternity Wing and special neonatal unit. At the time, obviously, we didn't realize the importance of this.

One significant thing, however, was that Jacqueline had had a Cesarean section with Alexander and we had hoped that she wouldn't have to have one again. In Kingston, the consultant made a decision to try for a natural birth. It was at about three or four o'clock in the morning on May 5, 1995—one month premature— that Jacqueline started going into labor. They weren't too worried that it was happening so early because twins are usually premature.

At about quarter to five in the afternoon she gave birth

Then I noticed the doctors were getting concerned.

to a little girl. I was watching the whole thing, which was marvelous. As soon as her head was out, she opened her eyes and looked around. After she was born, the little girl was bundled into a blanket and put into a warm crib. Then I noticed the doctors were getting concerned.

I looked at the heart monitor and realized that the heartbeat of the second baby had dropped right down to about 40 beats—it should be 140 to 160. He was barely alive. The doctor got quite annoyed with the midwife who had gone ahead with the natural birth.

He said, "Why didn't you go into surgery and get these twins out with a Cesarean?"

She said, "There was no need to."

And he said, "Well, what are we going to do now?"

I remember grabbing him by the shoulder and almost shouting, "We are going to pray!" He gave me the most extraordinary look. He was totally taken aback. He was just beginning to panic.

He said, "Quickly, give me the forceps!" The problem was that the second twin was breached. Meanwhile, I was quietly saying my prayer, which was not a complicated prayer. It was "Oh, God! Help!"

The man got the forceps and I was holding Jacqueline's hand, hardly daring to watch. I remember seeing this thing come out of Jacqueline. When the little girl had come out, she had been the right color and very animated. But this time what looked like a corpse came out of Jacqueline. There was no movement and he was a pale grayish-blue color. No sign of life whatsoever.

There was a very young pediatrician who was marvelous. He took the baby and put the baby right into an incubator and put the mask on. I carried on praying. Essentially, the problem was that his lungs were not working. They were completely filled with blood.

Afterward, we were told that the placenta had separated and his lungs had filled with blood so there was no oxygen getting to him at all. Gabriella had been born at 4:45 and he had come out at 5:03. For the whole of that time he had had no oxygen. They put the mechanical ventilator on him, but it couldn't force any air into his lungs. It just wasn't strong enough because they were totally saturated.

The sweat was pouring off the poor pediatrician and he was really working hard. He had gotten a set of bellows and was physically trying to force air into Daniel's lungs. For about 15 or 20 minutes they worked hard. I was just praying—I couldn't think of anything else—and I was comforting Jacqueline who couldn't see this and know what was going on. She did know there was a problem.

Two or three other doctors came. There were four or five people crowding around the incubator giving injections. Then they whisked the incubator out on wheels and disappeared. They took both babies. The midwife said, "Don't worry. They'll tell us what is going on."

Then we had the worst time. We got on to the phone and started telling everybody that the babies had been born. Jacqueline's father had come down from Northampton during the night and was staying at our house. He and Alexander came to visit after about an hour. But we had absolutely no news of the babies.

For about four or five hours we had no knowledge of what was happening to them. Nobody said anything to us. We kept saying, "Even if there is something wrong, we want to know and we want to see them."

Eventually we had a long talk with the midwife and said, "Look, it is very important to us that we are able to go and pray with our babies. Even if they die we want to go in there and pray with them." She understood that and persuaded the neonatal unit staff to allow us to come in. We were kept outside the cubicle where they were working. They had been operating on the boy for about five hours.

They had put a nasal-gastric tube through his nose in his stomach; ventilator tubing through his mouth into his trachea into his lungs. He had a saline drip and an alternate line for drugs. He had a cardiac monitor and another monitor to measure the blood gases.

He was very jaundiced and was under a special lamp.

He weighed 4 lbs. 15 oz., while the little girl was 4 lbs. 6 oz.

We watched as they were trying to get one of the lines into his belly-button and it was very difficult. Everything was swelling up and it was becoming increasingly difficult to get anything into him.

After a while the specialist came out to us and took us into a cubicle and said, "Look, the girl is going to be okay. She is a bit small, but she's going to be okay. Your son is not good. He didn't have oxygen for 23 minutes and that led to a number of other complications. His kidneys stopped working. We believe his liver has started to fail. His brain has swollen up. Basically, all the major organs have suffered traumatically as a result of the lack of oxygen." And he was also having fits by this stage.

We pressed him for some sort of prognosis and he said, "Well, at best, he has a 10 percent chance of surviving. But every minute he survives, that slightly increases his chances. If he survives the night, it is better." By this time it was 9:00 or 10:00 P.M.

That first night, Jacqueline and I spent the whole night sitting by

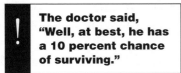

The doctor said, "Well, at best, he has a 10 percent chance of surviving."

his bed, looking at him through the glass, praying, talking to him, and encouraging him—just letting him know that we were there. Halfway through the night, we decided it was time we named him just in case he didn't survive. That was very important.

Before they had been born, we had had a short list of names including Maximilian, Charles, and a few others. But now, we each just prayed about it. As I was praying, I suddenly thought, "I know his name. His name is Daniel. How am I going to explain this to Jacqueline?" I remember looking at Jacqueline and saying, "Darling, I think I know his name." And she said to me, "I think I do too. It's Daniel, isn't it?"

It had not been on our short list of names—it was not a name that we had even considered—but we both just knew that it was Daniel. That night we read the whole Book of Daniel together.

Daniel survived the night.

The next day, which was a Saturday, we called Bruce and Geraldine Streather—our Alpha group leaders—and said, "Look, the babies have been born, but there are some significant problems with Daniel. Please will you pray." Marvelously, Geraldine and Annabel (her daughter) came to the hospital to see the babies and prayed with them and with us.

We feel that was a turning point in Daniel's recovery because until that point it had just been Jacqueline and me praying and now other people began to pray.

On Sunday—day three—I decided it was very important that I went to church. I went in a terrible state not knowing what to do and sat at the back of the church and just cried through the whole evening service. By now, we had been told that Daniel had a 50 percent chance of survival.

After the service I went to find Sandy and said, "We have this problem and I would be most grateful if you could pray for the babies." So Sandy prayed for me and for the babies. I was in such a state that I was crying all the time.

Jacqueline:

On that day, something rather unusual happened to me. The consultant who had been looking after me came up and said, "Listen Jacqueline, Daniel is going to be all right."

And I said, "What do you mean?"

He said, "I am not allowed to say this, but I just know that he is going to be all right." And I said, "How can you say that?" He said, "I have been to church and I have prayed for him and . . ."—he was almost crying, "I just know in my heart that he is going to survive.

But don't tell anybody else about this."

Later, I was spurred on to pray for a name for the little girl because the night before Alexander had said to the babies, "Good-bye, Daniel. Good-bye, girl."

I said, "You can't call her 'girl'."

He said, understandably, "Well, you haven't got a name for her."

So I started praying about it and I said, "God please give a name to this little girl." Then Gregory rushed in and said, "I know what her name is!" And I said, "So do I!"

And we both said, "Gabriella." We found out afterward, it means "woman of God."

When Geraldine had come to visit, she had given me a book called *My Dear Child* by Colin Urquhart and I started reading it. I remember reading the part about where he says that God doesn't inflict suffering on any of us and when we pray we can't expect an instant answer to our prayers. God is sometimes trying to tell us something.

I decided to give Daniel to God. I called to God and said, "Lord, I know that You can take Daniel at any time and if You do I will never feel angry about that. He is Your gift to me."

As soon as I started praying that I felt so much better. It was like a release and was very important to me. At the same time, I knew that he was important to God as well.

Gregory:

On Monday, we received a phone call from the church saying, "Tom Peek [*a member of the HTB pastoral staff*] will be coming to pray to represent the church." Tom came and we had a session praying for the babies. That was marvelous. It reinforced all the positive thoughts we had about HTB and the fact that we were part of a family and the family was caring. That was very important.

Daniel's progress continued. After a week Gabriella was allowed to come home. Daniel stayed for a second week. The chances of his survival were going up all the time.

The problem at this stage was what condition he would be in—because there was no indication. We were warned quietly that there was a possibility of a lasting effect, but that they wouldn't know that for a little while. Within another week, Daniel was home—very small and quite weak. It was marvelous to see him developing even more swiftly than his sister.

Jacqueline:

Daniel had a brain scan when he was about two months old. The specialist said that he couldn't say what the long-term complications would be, but there could be brain damage. He recommended physiotherapy for Daniel every day and I later gathered that he suspected some cerebral palsy because of his lack of oxygen.

His muscle movements were very, very tense so they wanted to loosen his muscles up. He went to hydrotherapy every week for quite a while. The physiotherapist was amazed at Daniel's recovery and it is now agreed there is no way he has cerebral palsy. All this has made my faith stronger. If anything happened to my children, it would devastate me, of course, but at the same time I know that these children are not purely my children. They are God's children. Knowing that, I think I can accept a lot more than I could otherwise.

Gregory:

I now feel very strongly that I am nothing more than a custodian. God has a plan for these children—otherwise he would not have allowed Daniel to survive. Our job is to get them to the point where they can fulfill their role for God.

Apart from some asthma directly resulting from his early medical condition, Daniel is now healthy and strong. "He is just the most wonderful confirmation of God's power," says Gregory.

He just said, "There's nothing we can do. You will be deaf for the rest of your life."

The story of Rachel Maylor

Rachel Maylor became deaf in her left ear in 1993 as a result of an infection. She had extensive hospital tests and was told that her inner ear had been irreversibly damaged and she would never hear through that ear again. Then, in November 1994, she attended a service at Holy Trinity Brompton with her father, Stephen. Here the two of them describe the extraordinary sequence of events that astonished her doctors.

Stephen's story:

My wife Sue and I met at the local Baptist church at Greenford. We have three daughters: Rachel, Sarah, and Louise. They have each made a commitment to the Lord.

My family and I arrived at HTB at the end of July 1994 after leaving our local church in Greenford in rather painful circumstances. Initially, we came to HTB after reading in the press about all that had been happening. We were looking for spiritual refreshment, rest and recuperation after what had been a difficult time.

In November 1993 my daughter Rachel, who was then 13 years old, had complained of a very sore ear. She came home from school and said her ear had been bleeding. Our GP examined her and could find no abnormality. Shortly afterward, on her way home from school, she collapsed in the street and was taken to Mount Vernon Hospital where the doctor diagnosed an infection.

Rachel subsequently told us that she wasn't able to hear properly and that started our visits to a number of different consultants. After Mount Vernon, we went privately to the Clementine Hospital in Harrow, where the consultant called in his colleague from Northwick Park Hospital, Harrow. It was then that we were told that the deafness in Rachel's ear was irreparable.

Later, it was recommended that she should go to St. Mary's, Paddington. Rachel had an audiometry test that confirmed profound deafness in her ear. We saw two registrars who simply confirmed that the original diagnosis was right. They explained that the damage was at the back of the ear, so a hearing aid would not help. That was when I suppose we accepted the inevitable.

One Sunday, Sue had a migraine and she said to me, "Why don't you go to the five o'clock service and take one of the children?" Rachel and Sarah decided they both wanted to go, so the three of us went. We had to sit up in the balcony because we couldn't get in downstairs—but we were blessed by the service and when there was an invitation for prayer, both the girls said they wanted to go forward. I went with them and asked a lady who was there to come and pray for them—a lovely American lady. She prayed for Rachel first and then for Sarah. Both ended up on the floor, slain in the Spirit. I was in tears praying over both of them with this lady and we went home on cloud nine.

A week later, on Sunday November 13, 1994, we all went as a family to the 5:00 P.M. service. Rachel said, "I want some more of this," and went forward again for prayer at the end of the service. What I didn't know was that Rachel had asked for healing. I was standing next to her when she started complaining of pain in her ear. I had a sense of what might be happening so I put my finger in her good ear and whispered in her deaf ear, "Can you hear me?"

Then, with a loud cry, she said, "Yes!"

We attended the hospital the following week as I wanted medical confirmation that the healing was complete. The audiometry test showed normal hearing in both ears. Rachel and I both broke down in tears when we saw the results and I explained to the lady who had done the test that I believed God had healed my daughter. She said, "Well, praise God! I am a Christian too!"

So we had a little praise meeting together there. The Hindu surgeon who saw her said: "I didn't know God was an ENT surgeon!" And I said, "Well, God created them!" Praise God who still performs miracles.

Rachel's story:

The doctor who first told me I was going to be deaf clearly wasn't very used to working with children. He just said, "There's nothing we can do. You will be deaf for the rest of your life." That's how he said it and then he walked out. Later, he came back in and started talking, but I was just in my own world.

I was really, really upset. I just felt really hurt and my world was falling apart. Getting used to it was hard work. I had to change places in class. My friends had to make sure they spoke louder. Sometimes I couldn't understand people and I had to see what they were speaking by reading their lips. I got used to that after a while.

I was prayed for at a service at Holy Trinity Brompton in July 1994 and was filled with the Holy Spirit. I started crying but I wasn't sad. I was happy. Even when I was in the car going home, I couldn't stop laughing. I was just so happy. Some of my friends at school were saying, "Why don't you go forward and ask for your ear to be prayed for?" I said, "No, no, no. It would just be very embarrassing and nothing will happen."

> **!** I had to change places in class. My friends had to make sure they spoke louder.

Then I went forward at a 5:00 P.M. service a couple of weeks later. I wanted to ask God if there was some reason why this had happened to me and if He could explain it to me. I went up there and I was feeling a bit worried. I'd only been forward once before. Then this lady named Victoria came forward.

161

First she asked me what I would like to be prayed for and I said that I'd like to be prayed for concerning the deafness in my left ear. She said, "Of course," and she started to pray for me. She said that she wanted the love of God to come over me and she wanted God to be with me. I just closed my eyes and concentrated fully on God. And all of a sudden things started to happen. First of all, I was just praying and I felt this peace. I felt really calm and happy. I couldn't hear what she was saying but I could tell that she was talking. I can't explain it. It was weird. I couldn't stop my hands shaking.

It wasn't as if I were making it up. It was really happening. Then I just closed my eyes and let God take over—and after a while I started getting pains in my ears. I fell over because the pain in my ear was just like a stabbing pain going on and on. I was screaming in pain. It was really, really bad in my left ear, my deaf ear.

I was rolling around in pain screaming, then I started to calm down. I was still shaking and Victoria was praying for me and she just said to me, "How do you feel?"

I said, "I feel a bit shaken, actually," and told her about these pains in my ear. She said, "Have you ever had these pains before?"

And I said, "No—and I don't really want them again."

She said, "Let's just pray for more healing and for the love of God to come over you."

And I said, "Yes, OK. Whatever you think." And so she prayed for me and I turned over and I didn't hear or think anything. I didn't have any pain after that."

Then I heard my dad speaking in my ear and I just answered him. He said, "Can you hear me?"

I said, "Yes, I can hear you."

He said again, "Can you hear me?"

And then I jumped up and started screaming and jumping around the church. I could hear him with my left ear. I couldn't believe it, I kept saying, "Dad, say something in my ear. Keep whispering. Just talk in my ear." It was incredible. Oh—it was just a wonderful feeling, I just can't explain it."

My relationship has become so much stronger. The Sunday after I went forward and asked my Dad to pray for me because I wanted to be thankful to God for what He'd done for me. Then the Holy Spirit came upon me and I was on the floor for nearly an hour. I couldn't stop shaking. I was fully aware of what was happening and my whole body was really violently moving. My dad had to carry me out in the end.

> **And then I jumped up and started screaming and jumping around the church.**

I was just thinking, "God, You're so wonderful." I was so thankful to God for what He was doing for me.

Some days later, we went back to the hospital for more tests. Dad said to the lady who was doing the tests, "We've got a surprise for you." Then we went to the consultant. He was a Hindu and said, "Yes, these things do happen now and again." When we got the tests back we compared the old one to the new one, I just couldn't control myself. I was so happy to see them. It was brilliant.

Rachel Maylor is currently studying for her college entrance. She remains a regular churchgoer and is a member of a "Youth Outreach" proclaiming the Christian faith in London clubs and halls through drama, singing, and dancing. "Since my healing, my life has been wonderful," she says.

> *"I alone know the plans I have for you, plans to bring you prosperity and not disaster, plans to bring about the future you hope for."*
> *Jeremiah 29:11*

8

"I felt this huge peace come over me. I felt really calm, as if all those worries that had bubbled up to the surface had been taken away."

The story of Robert Tincknell

To Robert Tincknell, it seemed a marriage "made in heaven" until his fiancée Rachel, with whom he had lived for a year, declared that her Christian faith must come first and she could not marry him. He assumed she was having an affair. Here Robert describes how his life was turned "upside-down":

I can remember going to church a couple of times when I was very small, but that was it really. The times when my parents took me, I could count on the fingers of one hand. My only real experience was at boarding school chapel, where I sat there twiddling my thumbs bored with the whole thing. Divinity classes and religious education were opportunities to have fun at the back of the class. I thought school was there completely for my entertainment, so when I left I didn't have many qualifications. The only thing I was interested in was doing the lighting for school plays, concerts, etc. So I came to London and banged on all the stage doors trying to get a job.

In the end, I got a job on *Time*—Cliff Richard's show on Tottenham Court Road. I was there for about 18 months, but it was clear that I wasn't going to make any money being a lighting operator, and at the time that was important to me.

My father had been successful in property development and construction and I think I always felt I had to match or better him. I decided to go to Leicester Polytechnic to study surveying. I did my three years getting a degree, and then did two years in the business—as a result of which I got my formal qualifications.

By this time it was the early 1990s and the building industry was in recession, so I worked for my father for a year or so while I was trying to get a job in London for a large firm of surveyors.

I sent out about 400 letters and got no response—not even an interview. I decided to target the companies I most wanted to work for. I wrote a letter to one managing director congratulating him on all his profits made in such difficult times and said, "I am desperate for a job, and I'm very good and determined at what I'm doing." I finished the letter, "Yours, hoping for an interview, Robert Tincknell."

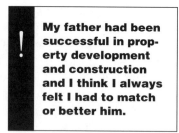

> My father had been successful in property development and construction and I think I always felt I had to match or better him.

He replied and invited me to his office for an informal chat. I did loads of preparation beforehand and went to meet him. After we had been talking for a while, I could sense he was going to bring it to an end and say something like, "We will keep your application on file" so I thought I would strike while the iron was hot.

I said, "I fully accept that you can't really tell what I am like in 10 minutes, so I am prepared to come and work for you for nothing for three months, then if you like me, you can take me on."

He sat back in his chair and smiled at me, and that was it! He said, "You can start on Monday." After three months, they took me on permanently. That was in 1992.

My life was quite hectic. I was living in Clapham with friends from school, partying and drinking. I was getting into work at 7:00 A.M. and leaving at 8:00 P.M. I was a workaholic during the day—my career was the most important thing in my life.

I met Rachel when she was at St. Thomas's Hospital training to be a physiotherapist. I always got along well with her, but she never stayed anywhere long enough for us to get to know each other better.

One night, she came to London to see a close friend of hers named Caroline, who later got married to an old friend of mine named Robin. Caroline and Robin set it up for Rachel and I to meet—and, sure enough, I was captivated by her.

Rachel had been a Christian since she was four and came from a very Christian family and I knew that she was heavily into her local church.

I had no interest whatever in church and I didn't want to be involved. The whole thing was totally alien to me and I wasn't sure I wanted to have a relationship with someone who had a faith that might have an effect on me. She was also concerned about my lack of faith—but we didn't talk to each other much about it.

Soon after this, Rachel slipped a disc and was in a lot of pain lying on her back for six weeks. She needed some help and suddenly there I was, driving down to Bath all the time.

Her small group from church didn't really help much and I offered a shoulder to cry on. Over a couple of months, she drifted away from her faith, which I was pleased about.

For a year we spent most of our lives on the freeway. Then Rachel decided to quit her job and move in with me. She got a job at the Royal Surrey County Hospital in Guildford and we got an apartment together in Thames Ditton. We lived happily that way for another year.

We knew her parents were not happy about the situation, but I didn't understand. What was so wrong with two people living together? Everyone was doing it.

> **!** **Over a couple of months, she drifted away from her faith, which I was pleased about.**

In August 1995, I asked Rachel to marry me and we got engaged. It was very exciting. We talked about how Rachel's faith would be involved in our marriage (although she wasn't going to church, she never felt she had fully lost her faith) and she agreed that if we had children, religion wouldn't be forced upon them and they would have a choice, which at the time seemed important to me.

Rachel then began having doubts. She felt God was telling her it was wrong for us to marry—which I didn't understand at all. So we decided it would be best if she moved out and spent a bit of time "speaking to God."

I thought it a bit odd, but I never thought it would keep us from getting married. Rachel moved in with Ken and Gill Morgan, some old friends of her parents, who are very kind people. I liked them a lot.

They are Christians and run a Crusader group in Virginia Water and help in the local church, both of which Rachel then began attending.

Then, about four to five weeks later, in September 1995, Rachel came to the apartment one night and I knew by the look on her face that all was not well.

I said to her, "You're not going to marry me are you?" And she said "No."

There were a lot of tears and I just said "That's it then"— and walked out of the apartment leaving her in there.

I drove into London and stayed with friends there for two weeks. I couldn't face going back to the apartment. I was furious that two people who loved each other and wanted to spend the rest of our lives together could no longer do so.

Rachel said that her relationship with Jesus was the most important part of her life and if we didn't share that relationship then our goals in life would be different. She was so peaceful when she talked about it that the only explanation I could come up with that fit the facts was that she was having an affair.

We didn't speak to each other for about three or four weeks, I was convinced it was all over. Then I was driving back from the west country with some friends and one of them had a bad back, so someone suggested popping in to see Rachel for some physiotherapy on our way back.

I really wanted to see her and it seemed like a good excuse. We dropped by and Rachel and I arranged to meet the following week to talk through how we were going to sort the situation out, if possible.

At this point my determination returned and I began to think of ways to get Rachel back. I decided to try to get someone whom Rachel respected to tell her that it was all right to marry me.

As a student, Rachel had spent three months living in the home of a couple called Nicky and Pippa Gumbel, who were friends of her parents. Nicky was apparently a clergyman at some church in Knightsbridge. So I decided to set up a meeting with this fellow Nicky Gumbel. I was sure that he would explain to Rachel that she was going a bit overboard and that it was fine to marry me.

Rachel and I went to the house—it was quite tense in the car—and we sat in the study with Nicky and Pippa and proceeded to tell them our story. Rachel was in floods of tears and so was I.

Every single argument that I had carefully planned, Nicky shot down in flames because he had so many logical and sensible arguments why our marriage wouldn't work and why it would be much better for us if I was a Christian as well.

> **At this point my determination returned and I began to think of ways to get Rachel back.**

I listened and somehow everything he said seemed to make sense. It made me realize that the reasons Rachel had left were perhaps genuine. Then Nicky asked me to an Alpha supper at Holy Trinity Brompton and I agreed. This was in December 1995.

On that night, Rachel and I sat in the car in the HTB parking lot and I really didn't want to go into the church. I thought I was going to find a lot of wet, sandal-wearing men and hippy women. I sat in the car smoking. I must have chain-smoked five cigarettes before I plucked up enough courage to go in.

I had only gone to church for weddings and funerals, so had never really been in church of my own choice. Rachel was so kind and patient and she had this huge peace over her, which was driving me insane!

When I walked in the door I was pleasantly surprised. Nicky came up and introduced us to couple called Nick and Debs whom we sat down next to for supper. It was amazing as they had been through a very similar experience to us.

Nick was a director of a large city firm and I thought, *Well, here is a normal guy, a director of a company who obviously does very well—and yet he comes here.*

I found Nicky's talk quite interesting. He was suggesting that people come on the Alpha course and I knew Rachel wanted me to go on the course. I looked around at the people there, the environment, the food and thought, *Well, I can handle ten weeks of this. I'll do it for Rachel.*

I felt that if I hadn't at least tried, I wouldn't be able to live with myself. I still thought that there was nothing to what they said, but I would do it to keep everybody happy.

The first night of Alpha was quite interesting. Rachel did the course with me and we were in Nicky Gumbel's group with a good bunch of people.

There was a guy in our group named David who was as cynical as I was about the whole Christian faith. David and I would sit in the corner every evening with our arms firmly crossed having a competition as to who could ask the hardest question.

I suppose it was into about week four that I started to think to myself, *This is quite interesting. This is quite a logical approach.* I started to listen closely and, to quote the Bible, "the scales started to fall from my eyes." I was starting to open up to the possibilities of the whole thing.

A few more weeks went by and we went on the weekend away at Pontins in Chichester. That was a real turning point for me. There was another guy in my group, Olly, and on the first night we got to bed at about two or three in the morning because we had a real party with some of the Pontin's staff dancing at the disco and having great fun. So I thought this was quite a good place.

On Saturday as we sat and listened to the talks, I felt like a champagne bottle being shaken harder and harder. At about seven o'clock, when Nicky asked for the Spirit to come, the cork finally flew off the bottle.

I felt the presence of God firmly. It was like all my pain and anguish over what had happened to Rachel and me had come right to the top. I was crying my eyes out and was in quite a state.

I felt Nicky tap me on the shoulder and ask me if he could pray for me. He put his hand on my back and I felt this enormous warmth come through my back. It was so warm that it was almost uncomfortable. It felt like there was a bar heater against my back. I will never forget it.

Then I felt this huge peace come over me. I felt really calm, like all those worries that had bubbled up to the surface had been taken away. I felt really peaceful, but also confused, because up until that point I had thought Christianity was a myth and Christians were wrong. Suddenly this happened and there was a possibility that it was all true. There was this massive confusion in my mind.

We had supper and I went straight to bed instead of going back to the bar, which for me was quite an event. I didn't sleep well at all with everything going over and over in my mind. I was still very, very confused.

We went back and I finished the rest of the course, by which time I really wanted God to come into my life. But, if somebody said "Are you a Christian?" I would say, "No." I wanted to take that leap of faith, but was still being held back by the skepticism and cynicism that I had had for 28 years of my life.

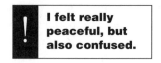

I felt really peaceful, but also confused.

I started reading my Bible in the evenings. It was difficult at first to read a book that for so long had just been fiction for me. It made little sense. I started saying prayers as well—mostly for understanding and guidance. I would just say, "God help me" and a prayer that Nicky often mentioned: "I believe. Help my unbelief."

I decided to do the next Alpha course and Nicky insisted that I come back as a helper. Rachel decided not to do it and, anyway, I wanted to do it on my own.

I went into Nick and Debs' group, which was great, but I remained very confused.

Then, some weeks later, Nicky and Pippa hosted a reunion of our first group. It was a summer lunch party and we were outside.

There, I managed to get Nicky to one side and asked him for some "Gumbel guidance." I said, "I am so confused, I just don't know what is happening. Am I a Christian or not?"

He simply said, "Do you pray?"

And I said, "Yes, every day."

He said, "Do you read your Bible?"

I said, "Yes, every day."

"Do you go to church on Sundays?"

"Yes, I wouldn't miss it."

"Are you enjoying the Alpha course?"

"Yes, I love it."

He looked at me and laughed, touched me on the shoulder and said, "Don't worry about it Rob. I think it will be all right."

At that point I suddenly got it and realized that, yes, I was there. The confusion was just suddenly lifted off. I had simply been confusing myself. I was thinking about it too hard.

I was really happy then. I was so alive. I felt my whole life had been turned upside-down—but I had this sense that it was now right-side up. I just felt really joyful. Someone said that it looked like I had been sleeping with a coat hanger in my mouth. I had this big grin on my face.

By now, I had stopped doing this just for Rachel's sake. For many weeks I had been doing it all totally for myself. But now I turned my attention back to Rachel and got down on bended knee once more and dug the ring out again.

> **!** Someone said that it looked like I had been sleeping with a coat hanger in my mouth. I had this big grin on my face.

From that point on, God totally blessed us in everything we did. We organized the wedding ourselves. I had debts from living it up in my younger days and Rachel didn't have any savings and suddenly all this money appeared.

We were married by Nicky Gumbel in front of 150 people at HTB on September 21, 1996. It was just a brilliant, an absolutely incredible day.

Everybody was crying—non-Christians and Christians. At the end we were singing "Amazing Grace" and there were five of us—Nicky, two friends (who had just read the prayers), and Rachel and I—standing together at the front of the church, all in tears. The Spirit just touched everybody that day and we were so blessed.

Very quickly after becoming a Christian, I was presented with a whole new set of goals. I became even more zealous for God than I was for my work. Also, my relationships with others have become extremely important to me—particularly the people on the Alpha course, as I feel closer to them.

I found myself caring enormously for people I had only known for a few weeks. My work is still as important to me, and I probably work harder than ever before, but I know where it fits into my life. My passion for God has first priority.

Having a relationship with God and being a part of a church community is just amazing. It sets you free from the trials of life. I now face difficult times at work with a spirit of optimism, rather than despair, because I know that God is standing by me and that He is going to look after me.

My relationship with Rachel is stronger now than I could ever have imagined it could be. It is so, so strong. It could never have been like that without God in it.

I feel normal now. I feel right. I feel right-side up. My relationship with God is the most important thing in my life. The second is my relationship with Rachel.

I still go down to the pub with my friends and we have a good laugh. I threaten to get them into an Alpha course and they say, "No way!" But I just continue to pray for them.

Robert and Rachel Tincknell attend a church near their home in Hambledon, Surrey, where they help to lead an Alpha course.

"I was close to my Dad. But my last words to him had been in anger. That was something that I struggled with for a long time."

The story of Andrew Gemmell

Andrew Gemmell was traveling in Australia when he heard the news that his father had died tragically while swimming on vacation. He was devastated and the experience made him discount any interest in the Christian faith. But then he met some friends who invited him on an Alpha course at St. Paul's, Onslow Square. Here he describes what happened.

My family used to go to church twice a year—the Easter and Christmas routine—but at my school, it was a drill of going six days out of seven for five years. It meant zilch. It was just ritual, there was no meaning behind it. I certainly never contemplated any relationship with God. It was just that you went in there, sang your hymns, listened to the lesson, listened to the talk. Then you went out again and that was it. It tended to last half an hour. A year after leaving school, I went to Australia to travel for six months, mostly on my own. On what was virtually my last day there, I received a message at my hostel in Adelaide to phone home urgently. I knew my parents were on a two-week vacation in Spain, but I phoned home at once. My sister answered the phone and broke the news to me that my father had drowned while on vacation. He had been swimming with friends and, being a stronger swimmer, had swum farther out than them. He wasn't miles out, but he swam out too far and there was a very strong riptide that swept him out. The others realized that he was in trouble and tried to get a boat, but the safety boat that was supposed to be there wasn't. So they went to the next bay and when they finally got it and came back, it was too late. They found his body.

When I heard this, I was just a wreck. I suddenly became incredibly friendless, with no one to turn to. I flew home immediately. Those 24 hours getting home were terrible. I was close to my dad, but my last words to him had been in anger. That was something that I struggled with for a long time. Father-son relationships can be quite tempestuous at times, and I think we had one of those relationships. But he did so much for me and I loved him to bits. I felt terrible that I'd had no opportunity at all to tell him how I really felt about him. For ages I remembered the arguments and the bad times. It just drove a wedge between me and any idea I'd had of God before. I still went to church twice a year—Easter and Christmas—and really didn't think much of it.

I had a difficult time when I went to Durham University two months later. Suddenly I was thrust into a different situation 300 miles from home and I felt I needed someone to talk to—a father or male. I had no brothers. There was no one there. But in the end I made a lot of good friends. By chance, my father had taken out AA insurance on the car, which we later discovered contained a little sub-clause about money for death insurance. So we received some money from that and my mother wanted to get us something special that Christmas. I got a very nice video camera, which was well beyond anything I had ever gotten for Christmas before. In hindsight, it is nice that something that she picked out for me in remembrance of my father is something that set me up in my future career.

After leaving the university, I joined a firm of stockbrokers in the city. In my spare time I was running a disco making a couple of videos. I did a couple of friends' weddings and they came out particularly well. A friend of my mother's, who was quite a well-known photographer, saw them and said, "I could send you out to do a couple for me when people call me up." So I did that. Then he said half-jokingly, "If you ever get to the point where you want to start a business with a partner, come and talk to me." But I stayed with my stock brokerage firm and started taking my exams.

At around this time, I heard about a dance called Ceroc and began going to classes. I went along for a bit of a laugh. Then I decided that I would like to make a teaching video for James Cronin, who was in charge. I went up and spoke to him. We found we had a lot in common, in that we had both been involved in the disco business and had the same sort of background. We ended up chatting quite a bit. He said, "I would really like you to make a promotional video. There are these four events that I would like you to cover." I was still working for my stock brokerage company and making videos in my spare time.

We made the video and used a song called *Sing Hallelujah* by Dr. Alban as the backing track. It was a song that seemed to keep coming up when I danced with Janie Cronin. One night in 1994, I was watching a TV program on something called stigmata, where people bleed from their hands or feet or head or side—like Christ—for no reason at all. It seems to happen especially around religious festivals. I was absorbed by it. When it came to the end, I thought, *Wow, what a powerful program. I wonder if there is anything to this whole spiritual thing?*

I went to bed that night and had a very vivid dream that I was back at school standing outside the chapel, watching everyone come out with the same attitude that I had when I was there. For some reason or other, I was saying, "No, no, no. You have got to stop. You have got to listen. You have got to go back and actually take note of what is going on in there because there is something more to it." I had a really strong image of the real presence of God in that dream.

At that point I had an immensely strong image of my father, and this was not a dream, I know it wasn't. He was standing on the steps. I went up and I just held him. I knew then not to use him as a dividing wedge between me and God. I was in bed asleep when this happened. It was very, very strong—very, very powerful. As I held him, I felt a mutual warmth. It was incredibly emotional. He put his arms around me. I felt, "I have got to do something about this. I have got to make inquiries."

I knew that James Cronin and his wife Janie were involved with church, but I had no idea what it was about or anything like that. I had thought, *Well, that's a shame because I quite like them, really.* The next evening, I went to Ceroc and caught Janie walking out. I stopped her and said, "Janie, I am really sorry to stop you, but something has happened to me and I need to know what I can do about it." At the time I just thought it was perfectly normal to ask someone who went to church all about personal experiences. I told her all about what had happened to me and she told me about the Alpha course.

> **For some reason I was saying, "No, no, no. You have got to stop. You have got to listen.**

She explained that it was a ten-week course to learn about Christianity without committing yourself to anything. It sounded like a very good idea. I believed I was intellectually capable enough to make a relatively informed judgment and, after ten weeks make a decision as to what I wanted to do. I went to Alpha at St. Paul's Onslow Square, and after the first night I thought, *This is interesting.* At the end John Peters does a prayer where you can commit yourself to God, if you think that that is what you are ready for. I thought, *No way! I am here to make a decision after a ten-week course.*

That night, I was lying in bed thinking about some other things that had happened to me that week:

• I had had my car broken into and $2,000 worth of uninsured video equipment stolen.

• Our house had had a burglar alarm fitted and the guy who was fitting it, while putting in one of the infrared detectors, had drilled

179

through a water pipe and flooded the front room.

- My TV had blown up.
- I had food poisoning for a day.

I was lying in bed thinking of other friends who are Christians and who had told me what their experience of life with God is. I thought, *If there is a God, then why wait? However, if there is no God, then what am I losing anyway by praying to a non-entity?*

So, I thought that I would pray the prayer. I had taken careful note of the prayer John had prayed at Alpha and I said it that night. I prayed along the lines of: "Lord forgive me for what I have done in the past to offend You. I want to change. I want to follow Your Word. Lord Jesus, come into my life and change it and transform it." It was a very simple prayer.

The following Friday, I decided to go to Ceroc at St. Paul's to see James and Janie. On my way there I was listening to the radio when I began thinking about God and suddenly thought of my prayer that I had said on Wednesday night. I wondered, "Have I just fallen for the emotional trap? Have I actually been sensible about this?"

I was faced with the question: would people see me as being stupid and just following the trends? I said, "Well, God I need to know now whether I have made a mistake or whether I really have actually committed myself to Someone who is personal and knows my thoughts." Within ten seconds, without a DJ interlink on the radio, *Sing Hallelujah* came on the radio. The whole previous couple of months resolved into a resounding, "Yes, this is right!" I sat in the car, driving along just south of the river, and I was in tears.

After this I was very open to the talks. I still wanted to make an intellectually-based decision. I still wanted the facts. I was changing. I was definitely changing. I was still working in the city and finding it increasingly hard. I was in quite a prominent position and finding it difficult to lie while I was dealing. Sometimes you had to lie in order to get better prices and increase your profitability. You might lie about having a client wanting to buy a whole load of stock, when there is nobody there at all. You might say to a broker, "I need a really special favor here . . ." when in fact you are just trying to con him. I felt compromised between my new-found faith and things that I was sometimes doing at work.

At first my family thought I was joining a cult. But one incident certainly helped to ease that. When I was seven years old, I had cut my wrist incredibly badly when I put my hand through a plateglass window. I had almost died and lost just over half my body's blood supply. They managed to mend my hand, but one thing they said I would never be able to do was to move my little finger.

I had cut a tendon, a nerve, and an artery and the cut to the tendon meant that my hand was in a claw-like grip. I used to play the piano with my fingers wrapped. Gradually they unfolded a little, but certainly my little finger wouldn't move. My whole family knows about my hand. After becoming a Christian, I had prayed to God for the healing of my little finger so that I could show Mom and my whole family why I believed what I believed in. This was a long-standing prayer.

By this time I was helping to lead a group on Alpha. The evening on healing came along and I was praying for someone when John said from the front, "There is a piano player with a damaged right hand." At that moment, I felt a twinge in my little finger, and I thought, *Aha!* I went up to John and said, "I think that is actually for me. Would you mind praying for it?" So he did. This was just before Christmas 1995.

I then had an incredibly busy period over Christmas and I didn't go to church because I was just busy, busy, busy. Nothing else happened. I came back in January or February to do the next Alpha course. On the first week we were starting to pray. It was the first time I had seriously gotten down and prayed to God for quite awhile. I looked at my hand and the little finger was beginning to move. I went up to John and said, "I don't know what this is, but I have the feeling that something is happening here."

So he prayed for it again. Basically, over the next month my little finger was able to move virtually all the way in. This is after 15 years of being completely dead and the muscles completely wasted away. I told my mom and she was completely flabbergasted. She just didn't understand it. She still can't explain it to this day. What it did do is to help her understand the reasons why I am a Christian.

I decided to leave my job in stocks, where I was not happy. I had always been interested in doing videos and discotheques and the opportunity of doing it full-time just thrust itself upon me. A friend and I set up "The Last Word" partnership in April 1995, for which I do wedding videos—or celebrational videos. I also do short corporate stuff, promotional material. The latest thing that I have done is the Afghanistan video, for Children in Crisis.

God has answered so many prayers. I have had a physical healing. Whenever anything goes wrong, I am always now going back to my foundation, my roots, which is knowing that there is a God and there is more to life and that all I need do is rely on God. The whole issue of anger towards my Dad has been completely resolved. I now look at death in a completely different way. I am not frightened of death. I can reconcile death, which was a big thing for me in relation to my father's death.

I can honestly say that since I have become a Christian I have never felt depressed. I have always held on to the fact that there is much more to what we think of life. You have a constant Companion. You have got a constant Friend. Someone to turn to in times of need— Jesus.

Andrew Gemmell now attends Christ Church in Fulham. Following the growth of his video business, he is about to set up a film production company, "Cornerstone Films," with another Christian, Matthew Hemsley.

"I was totally into myself, the girls, and having a good time."

The story of Bernie Keane

London cab driver Bernie Keane had been a church-goer—on and off—for much of his life when he heard about the Alpha course at Holy Trinity Brompton. He and his wife Pamela decided to attend the course in October 1996. Here he explains how his attitude toward God, and life in general, has totally changed.

I was born in Saint Stephen's Hospital on Fulham Road and was brought up in the Kensington and Chelsea area. When I was one year old I got whooping cough, which led to spells in a children's hospital during my early years and left me with something called bronchiectosis. I was brought up in a strict Roman Catholic household. I became an altar boy at about nine years old. Later, I went to church on Sunday, but if I could get out of it, I would.

I left school at 15 and became a carpenter. Then I decided I did not want to do that and then got into seafood sales in New King's Road. I quit that, though, because a girl-friend said, "I like you, Bernie, but I don't like the smell of you.'

As a teenager in the sixties, I was in with a rough crowd. Every weekend we used to drive down to Brighton, stay there for the weekend, sleep on the beach, get drunk, and drive back. I was totally into myself, the girls, and having a good time. I carried on until I was over 30. I was drinking and clubbing—but to me I was having a good time. Later I managed a bookshop on Cromwell Road, where I met my lovely wife Pamela, who was working in the shop next door.

I stopped going to church when I was a teenager. It wasn't until I met and married Pam that I took an interest in going to Mass and visiting her church in Scotland—Pamela is Scottish. This slowed me down to a proper pace of lifestyle.

My first experience with Christianity from a different perspective was when I met a Greek shipping magnate who had become a Christian. He invited me to go and hear a missionary in a church hall over in Southwark, where there were a lot of vagrants. It was a marvelous sermon and at the end of it he asked anybody who wanted to be saved to stand up. I stood, but I didn't really understand it. I always have fond memories of the guy because I feel that he planted the first seed of Christianity in me.

To be a London cabbie involves learning all the streets and prominent buildings in London. It takes two to three years if you are good and you work hard at it. I used to get on my bike and ride around London every afternoon and then I would go off to night school in the evening. Weekends would be spent reviewing with a friend—calling out all the streets parrot style. To start off, they give you 600 runs, which all zigzag across London. You have to learn these 600 runs, picking up streets and points along the way. It's like a jigsaw.

The first night I went to night school, I thought, *This is impossible,* but your knowledge builds up—that's why they call it "The Knowledge." I took 14 exams to be a cab driver. For every 12 people who start The Knowledge, eight quit. In 1985, I became a cab driver and I have been one ever since.

When my daughter, Laura, was born, she was baptized Roman Catholic. I felt I had to give her some lead in faith. I started taking her to church. My wife used to come with me sometimes. We also attended my wife's church when we were in Scotland.

About 10 years ago, we went to a Billy Graham event at Earl's Court and I was fascinated by it. At the end I went down to the front and went up to one of the counselors with labels. We started talking and it was amazing. Of all the thousands of people there, he had a daughter in the same school and the same class as my daughter. I had a nice chat with him and he said, "Why don't you join a Bible class?"

I went to the Bible class he recommended but, looking back on it now, I wasn't ready then. I stopped.

I carried on going to the Catholic church with my daughter, sitting at the back. I was just going through the motions. The only bit of the service I used to enjoy was when they read the Gospel, gave the notices, and when we shook hands. The rest was a long drawn out ritual to me.

In the summer of 1996, Pamela and I went on vacation to Spain. We have some friends who have retired there. While there, they told us they had become Christians and they took us to a prayer meeting up in the mountains led—through a translator—by a couple of Colombian missionaries. These people had given up everything in Colombia and I was fascinated. At the end of the evening they invited people to come forward and be blessed. They would put their hands on people and pray for them.

Then the daughter of my friends said, "Read this psalm, Bernie. I always read this when I am a bit low or down and it gives me great strength." It was Psalm 139 ("O Lord, you have searched me and you know me. You know when I sit and when I rise . . ."). I read it. It was wonderful. She said, "Why don't you go and have the blessing?" I thought, *I am up in the mountains. It is the nearest I am going to get to God!* So I went in there and had a blessing. People prayed for me for quite awhile.

I felt these people were very genuine and real—and very, very committed to God. I was interested in becoming part of them.

I started chatting with my friend afterward and she said, "When you go back, why don't you and Pam do the Alpha course?" I asked what it was all about. They gave me a copy of *Alpha News* and I read a little bit about it. I came back and saw that there was one in

Wimbledon and one in Richmond, where my wife works. Then I read that Nicky Gumbel did one at HTB. I thought, *Let's go and see the top man. Let's go and do it with the top dog.* My wife said she could drive from Richmond and I was in town with my cab anyway. It worked out fantastically. We started the course in October 1996.

On the first night I walked in and thought, "Wow!" I was expecting a little village hall atmosphere with about 40 people. I never expected it to be 500 people. I sat down and had the food and thought that it was very nice, but I remember saying to myself, *Oh my word, it's a bunch of middle classes having a cozy little chat about Jesus over a casserole.* I always finish things I start, though, and after a couple of weeks, I relaxed and started enjoying Nicky's talks and relating to them greatly. I was very pleased with the group I was in too.

After about three or four weeks I was really getting into it. My wife and I would go home at night and sit up until one o'clock chatting about it all. I found it very amusing that we were going to stay at Pontins for the weekend. The Holy Spirit has always been a big thing for me and I was looking forward to it.

On Saturday, Nicky started talking about the Holy Spirit and I said, "Lord, I am trying to be sincere, please fill me with the Holy Spirit." I have always felt spiritually very hollow. Nothing happened.

On Sunday morning, I prayed again and suddenly felt a calmness over me. I felt a smile coming on my face. I felt so wonderful that there aren't any words to do it justice.

The only way I can describe it is that I got rid of all that guilt and all the hang-ups I had about religion. I just felt, for the first time in my life, that I had a relationship with God. I always wondered what people meant when they said, "I have a relationship with God" but I felt then I had a relationship with God. My wife says she has noticed a big change in me.

I read my Bible every day now. I wouldn't have done that before. My wife has just bought me a big Bible for my 50th birthday. It has got a lot of references in it and I find it very helpful. I can't get enough of it. I have to stop myself reading it because my wife keeps reminding me that I have got other responsibilities, like going to work and doing a few jobs around the house!

I now have a relationship with Jesus. I can talk to Him. Before I was always asking Him for things, but I spend more time thanking Him now. I thank Him for what has happened during the day, what has happened in my life. He has strengthened my marriage.

My sister-in-law accuses me of joining the God Squad and the guys down at the pub say I have become the Tambourine Man—but they all want to know what is going on.

I now go to an evangelical church in the same road that I live in—Worple Road, Wimbledon. I was just amazed at the fellowship when I walked in there, just the friendliness of the people. I have since thought back to all those years of going to church. I was trying to get to know God, but didn't know how.

I keep *Why Jesus?* and an Alpha pamphlet in the cab and sometimes I say to passengers, "Go along and try it. It doesn't cost you anything. It is like 10 evenings out at the theater! And you get a nice meal for £2.50."

I think Alpha taught me how to have a relationship with God. I talk to God now. I get on my knees every day—I would never have done that before.

Bernie Keane and his wife are still regular churchgoers near their Wimbledon home. Bernie helps out with a soup run for the homeless delivering meals around the center of London in his taxi.

> "God is our shelter and strength, always ready to help in times of trouble."
> *Psalm 46:1*

9

"I have never felt bereft."

The story of Zilla Hawkins

On July 22, 1996, Mick Hawkins, on staff at Holy Trinity Brompton, died of a sudden heart attack at the age of 42. He left a widow, Zilla, and six children. Around 600 people attended his funeral. Here, Zilla Hawkins gives an account of how she has clung to God's promises.

I was brought up a churchgoer. I had very high church parents, particularly my mother, who had a horror of evangelicals. She died when I was 22. My father was very much a churchgoer, a very fine man, and he was devastated (not surprisingly) by my mother's death.

By that time, I was living and working as a secretary in the Lord Chamberlain's office in London. It deals with all the main royal ceremonies and occasions—like royal weddings and funerals—and also administers Windsor Castle and Holyroodhouse. It was a fascinating job—great fun. I loved it. I went to church intermittently, but it became more and more sporadic.

Then, at the age of 24, I met Mick. I was sharing an apartment

189

with a girlfriend and we had a vacancy for a third person, which we advertised in *The Times*.

A man answered the advertisement and we decided to give him the room, which was rather out of the ordinary in those days. People didn't have coed apartments then—it was so long ago!

After we told him, the guy said, "I will move in on Monday and I will bring somebody with me to help me carry my luggage."

My girlfriend and I decided that we would cook dinner to welcome the new arrival, and we would cook enough for four—so if we liked the look of the luggage-carrier we would invite him to stay as well. He passed the test and that was Mick. That was how we met. His friend continued living with us and became a very good friend. He is Alice's godfather.

Then we started going out and got married a little over two years later. We were very excited to have a church wedding at the Queen's Chapel in St. James' Palace, where I worked. After we were married, we used to go to church at Queen's Chapel. We didn't go every Sunday, but we went most weeks, probably more often than not. It was a very conventional service.

When Alice was born in 1979, Mick was very struck by the whole business of birth and new life and this tiny little person who was so perfect. I think he was very blown away by it. He worked in insurance at Lloyd's and two weeks later he was there waiting for an underwriter when he met Gordon Scutt, who ran his own brokerage firm in Lloyd's.

Gordon is an out-and-out evangelist—he doesn't care what he says to anybody—and Mick told him about Alice. I think Mick said, "I have just had an amazing experience! I have just had a daughter and can't believe it." They then talked for about two and a half hours.

Gordon said, "You must come to St. Helen's Bishopsgate [*a church with a powerful evangelistic ministry among city workers*] with me. I will meet you outside the church next Tuesday for the lunchtime service."

Mick went along as arranged—but Gordon wasn't there. In the end, he went in and attended the service by himself. Dick Lucas [*Rector of St. Helen's*] was preaching and he said, "I wonder why any of you might have come here for the first time today? Perhaps something amazing has happened in your life. Perhaps you have just had a baby or something." Mick thought, *He is talking to me!*

He went the following week to St. Helen's and felt that it was speaking to him as well. Soon afterward, he was ill and stayed at home. During that time, he read John Stott's book *Basic Christianity*. He is not a reader—he only read about five books in his entire life, I suppose—so it was pretty amazing.

When he finished the book, he got down on his knees and gave his life to God. He was completely filled with it all and came and told me, "I have done the most amazing thing!"

I was furious! I was so angry. I kept saying, "How can you say you have been converted? We went to church—it is not as if you were a Muslim or something. You can't do this to me."

I thought he had gone off his rocker. He had always been one for great enthusiasm and I thought it was another one of those.

He kept saying to me, "Read this verse in the Bible" and "We have got to go to a different church." I was very upset because he seemed to have changed. I didn't want to read that bit in the Bible.

Somebody—I think it was Gordon—was very wise and said to him, "Just leave her alone. Don't say anything at all. Just look after her and love her." And he did.

It is much more difficult to go to church with a baby and so we started going to one around the corner from our home in Clapham—St. Luke's in Ramsden Road. The vicar came to see us and I said, "My husband says he has just been converted." He didn't say that he would probably soon get over it, but he did imply it was "not the sort of thing we do here."

A couple of months later, Mick brought home a brochure about a Christian house-party-week-away and he said, "Just thought you might like to look at this."

> Somebody—I think it was Gordon—was very wise and said to him, "Just leave her alone.

I bluntly refused and said, "I am not going! It says: 'Bring your Bible, bring your tennis racket, bring your swimming gear.' I hate swimming. I hate tennis. Nothing wrong with the Bible."

Anyway, we went. I don't know why.

Mick knew someone named Pippa Gumbel very well since childhood, having been brought up in the same area. So in getting to know Mick I had also come to know Pips and her husband Nicky.

This house-party-week was held in Bedfordshire and Nicky and Pippa were on the host team. Every evening I would come out from supper and there would be Nicky bouncing a soccer ball, "How are you Zilla? Everything all right?"

"No!" I said.

I was used to the Queen's Chapel and robes. And dignity. Yet here there were guitars. Heresy! It was the pits. At the end of the week Nicky and Mick sat me down with David MacInnes [*an evangelist, now Rector of St. Aldate's, Oxford*].

I said, "I don't understand it and I don't see why people keep saying that I have to be converted. I hate all this praying aloud."

He just said, "That's how they always used to pray in the old days, way back."

"But I still don't see why I have got to be converted. I am not a Buddhist. I go to church."

He replied, "Why don't you go over in ink what has been written down in pencil?" So I said, "Oh, all right!"

I suppose it was pride by that stage that was stopping me and he gave me a way out. Within the limits of what I understood at the time, perhaps I was a Christian, but there was so much more. It was not so much like an about face but more like getting off a bicycle and into a sports car. It was that kind of analogy.

I realized that if I said I believed in God and He was as amazing as I wanted Him to be, then to treat Him as anything other than the most important thing in my life was actually wrong.

So David MacInnes prayed with me, thanking God for showing me the way forward and asking Him to go with me from now on.

> **I suppose it was pride by that stage that was stopping me and he gave me a way out.**

After that, Mick and I started going to HTB. It did take a little bit of time for me to get used to the guitars. I like classical music and I love choirs and anthems—but HTB was great.

Nicky and Pippa were running a Bible Study group and I liked them very much. We had asked Pippa to be Alice's godmother. I remember the first time I met Nicky, he was so full of life.

But it was a horrible ten months, I have to say, from when Mick made that first announcement to me. I feared Mick might have become a nut and if that had happened it would have been very difficult for the years ahead. But then I became a loony too!

We did an HTB course called *Lighthouse* with Patrick Whitworth. It was a bit more academic than Alpha and we had to write an essay every week on some deep spiritual topics which was agonizing. Mick loved it. It was a super course to take and it lasted a year. Through that we made many more friends.

Then we continued to lead groups until we went to Sweden because Mick's job took us there. I had had three babies by this stage—Alice, Hannah, and Martha.

I had originally wanted to go but when we went out to take a look it was very depressing. It is beautiful and clean and the people are civilized. But they are very cold and the weather was incredibly cold. It was the coldest winter since 1942 and the first time that the Baltic Sea had frozen completely over. It snowed for five months. I had three young children.

I was pregnant when we went to Sweden and three months after we arrived I gave birth to the baby. He was a breech baby so I was given an emergency Cesarean.

When I came out of the anesthetic, Mick was there. He was in tears and told me we had a boy but he was very ill. That was the first I knew.

Later, they took me in an ambulance so that I could see him.

George lived for ten hours. He had something called Potters' Syndrome, which means that he had no kidneys. He never would have survived but we didn't know that at the time of the birth. He was baptized by the Swedish hospital chaplain.

It was quite tough because we had no friends. We had been going to the English church which was basically dead. People were so sweet but there was no life there at all and we couldn't find anyone who felt like us. Although, there were one or two.

The prenatal care out there is very good and you have your own midwife, whom you see every time. She was very sweet and she spoke English.

After I had given birth to George, we went back to see her and she suddenly looked at me and said "Can I ask you something?"

I said, "Yes."

She said, "Are you a Christian?"

I said, "Yes," and she replied, "So am I. I thought you must be."

It was amazing that God's provision had given me a Christian midwife. That was very rare. It was an extraordinary confirmation of God's provision and care.

Friends came from England to see us. Rupert Charkham [*now Vicar of St. Paul's, Salisbury*] came the next day. He was a great friend of Mick's through Lloyd's. He was up at Wycliffe Theological College along with Nicky and Pippa at that time.

When he arrived, Rupert told me that he had been to his principal to ask permission to come and Nicky had said, "Don't worry about the money. I'll arrange that."

Nicky then went to the bank and said, "I want all the Swiss Francs that you have." So Rupert turned up in Sweden with Swiss Francs instead of Swedish Kroner. In reality he didn't have a cent. I remember laughing and laughing about it.

We felt incredibly supported even though we were miles from anywhere. Mick's mother came, as did Patrick Whitworth [*then curate of HTB*]. Ken Costa paid for him to come and perform the funeral. Ken just called up and said "Who do you want out there?"

We never felt abandoned. From the moment Mick told me George was so ill, I was constantly aware of that verse in Genesis about Abraham and Isaac where God says "Because you have not withheld your only son, I will bless you." I really held on to that.

We supported each other, and when you have other children life has got to go on. That was the mercy of it. If he had been my first, it would have been much worse. The children were very sweet. Everybody was very kind.

We were in Sweden for another 18 months. Tilly was born there, almost exactly a year after George was born. At that stage we were still going to this dead church. The children brought life to the place. They got all those old dears on our side. We were trying to run a group and the vicar would come along from time to time. He would change the subject to something incredibly boring. It was tricky.

In July 1986 we returned to London. Mick's work couldn't find a replacement for him so he had to commute from Sweden for four months. That was a very dreary time. He came back for weekends.

We settled back into HTB. It was wonderful to be back. William was born in 1987 and then Rupert in 1990.

Originally, I had always thought we would have four children. After the end of our Lighthouse course, we were commissioned in the evening service and went up and were prayed for. At the time we had two children, but Nicky came and prayed for us and said laughingly, "I pray that you bless Mick and Zilla, Lord, and all their six children." We sort of said, "Don't be silly."

After we returned from Sweden, we were at a house party and were asked to tell the story of George and how God had supported us. The next day somebody there came up to me and said, "I was praying about you this morning and I felt God saying that George wasn't going to be your only son and that you were going to have another one."

When I found I was pregnant again I thought, *It must be a boy.* And it was. It was William.

Having had William, we thought that was our six children that Nicky had prayed for. Then we had Rupert.

The children have all joined in the life of the church in a big way. They love going to church, which is wonderful.

In July 1996, we went to Home Focus [*the teaching vacation week in July for HTB's "family" of churches in Pakefield, Suffolk*]. It seemed like a normal Focus and Mick just loved it. It was tremendous fun.

We were all there except Alice who was in Borneo doing the World Challenge Expedition—going through the jungle.

We arrived, set everything up. Everything was going fine, the weather was great. On Monday afternoon, Mick, who was a very good squash player, went off to play squash with Nicky. And that was the last I saw of him.

I had had absolutely no idea at all at any stage that there was anything wrong. He hadn't ever mentioned that he felt a bit off. The first I knew was when Hannah came running up to the chalet.

She was in tears.

She said, "Daddy's had a heart attack."

I said, "Don't be silly. Of course he hasn't."

Then Tricia Neill [*administrator of the Focus vacation*] came around the corner. She said, "We have just heard that Mick had been playing squash and has had a heart attack. Will you come?"

I said, "Sure."

Someone said that they would look after Rupert. I just got in the car with Trish and Emmy. We drove to the squash club parking lot and as soon as we drove in I knew what had happened because I saw a police car.

Nicky was there in a flood of tears. I remember thinking, *I knew this would happen* because you hear these stories about people who play squash. And then we went upstairs to the squash club bar and had a glass of water.

The policeman was there and asked, "Has he been ill at all?"

"No."

"Have you any idea why this happened?"

"No."

Then we went back to Pontins. Everybody looked the same. It was so odd that people look exactly the same and your whole life has completely changed in the space of 45 minutes.

I just thought, *What am I going to do?*

I had to tell the children. People found them and they came in one at a time. And then it was just a sort of blur, really.

It was so lovely to be there though. If it had to happen it could not have happened in a better way. He was all right—there was no growing old or getting ill. Everybody was there and were so, so kind. I was totally surrounded by people who cared and that did feel very much like God's provision.

It could have been two weeks later when he was due to go on a bike ride with Hannah from Land's End to John O'Groats. It could have happened in the wilds of the Scottish Highlands with just her. That would have been just awful.

There were certain verses that were absolutely key at that time. Someone gave me the verse from Romans: "Who shall separate us from the love of Christ?" I put that in the announcement in the paper.

Somebody else gave me three verses out of 2 Timothy: "For I am already being poured out like a drink offering, and the time has come for my departure. I have fought the good fight, I have finished the race, I have kept the faith. Now there is in store for me the crown of righteousness, which the Lord, the righteous Judge, will award to me on that day—and not only to me, but also to all who have longed for his appearing."

It is so beautiful. We were all in tears about it because it was so right. So that was very special. But in a funny way what I found so odd and very hard to handle was that I kept waiting for a particularly special verse like the one I had had when George died. And I didn't feel I had gotten it. They were wonderful verses but I didn't feel they were speaking to me in the same way.

I felt very much that I had to hang onto God's promises because that was the only thing to do.

One promise that bothered me was the one attached to the commandment about honoring our father and mother: "Honor your father and your mother that your days may be long." It is the first commandment with a promise. I was really bothered by it because Mick had been amazing to his mother. I thought, *If God is not going to keep this promise, then why should He keep any of His others?* I saw J. John [*a prominent British evangelist*] during the holidays and asked him why.

He replied, "I don't know, but we do know that 'all things work together for good for those who love the Lord.' " So I made sure that I hung to that verse.

At the time, I couldn't see how what happened could possibly be good. I didn't understand how it could be good for me and my children to be left without a husband and a father.

I began to feel that perhaps it was because I had always taken refuge behind Mick. I had always let him take the lead and do everything and felt relieved that I didn't have to do it—but perhaps through this God was going to make me stand on my own feet and do things in my own right for myself. It would in the end probably be good for me—even if I didn't like it.

That has happened now. So therefore it was good even though it was hard.

Sometimes I think for the children that it is a pretty unfair thing to do to your father when you are six and eight. Once again you have to go to God's promise "He will be a father to the fatherless" and believe it.

I think that is the hardest thing. I have just got to believe it even if it doesn't seem possible, because there is nothing else to do.

Mick's father had died when he was six. And Mick ended up perfectly normal. It hadn't apparently had any adverse effect on him. So that is an encouragement. He had always had a deep conviction of God's presence.

Every single moment I am conscious of the fact that Mick is not there. It is not a thing that ever goes out of my mind. Sometimes I'm unsteady and it is worse, but it is not something that I am ever unaware of.

One thing that people sometimes say to me is, "He will always be with you. You will always feel him by your side." That is one of the things I cringe at because he is not. I know where he is. On the whole, it is not something Christians say.

On the other hand, I love it when people talk about him and tell me about funny things he did. I don't want to forget him or want other people to either. I am aware of people being uncomfortable, but it is much worse for them than it is for me. I don't mind at all.

Although it is still so immediate to me, it is now history to most people. I don't want people to be inventing reasons to talk about him but I certainly don't want to avoid him in conversation.

People were enormously helpful in a practical way in the weeks following Mick's death. One of the most helpful things was when men or boys came and took the boys to play football.

I worried about that a lot because Mick used to play a lot with them. For a while I went out on to the Common and tried to kick a football, but then I thought, *This is not me.*

I love it when people talk about him and tell me about funny things he did.

Mick used to take a tennis racket and ball onto the Common and hit enormously high catches for the children. They loved it. But my little lob didn't get anywhere!

The children have been so incredible, particularly the older ones. They have looked after me, rather than the other way around. Alice writes me verses and puts them on my pillow.

One of the things I miss so much is the encouragement. Mick was one of the greatest encouragers there ever was. But the children are inheriting it. Occasionally it hits them that Daddy is not going to see them in their school play. He won't be there. And I think it is hard for them when people at school are talking about their parents.

They are all so different. Each of them has gone through it on a different level. There is very much a feeling of being in it together.

I have never felt bereft. I have always felt that God has been very close to me. Sometimes I have found it very hard to read my Bible but at the same time I haven't felt the hand of accusation. There has just been a closeness.

I have never felt anger or bitterness, which is once again part of God's provision. It may sound smug but I have always felt how fantastically good it is for Mick. I can't wait to be there myself.

The month after Mick died, we suddenly got some flowers on the front doorstep. And it has happened every month since.

One midterm, the doorbell rang and outside there were seven enormous bunches of roses left on the doorstep, named for each one of us, but with no indication of whom they were from. The card just said "Love and blessings."

I wasn't aware at first that the flowers always arrived on the 22nd—the day Mick died. But now I have realized that on the 22nd of every month a plant or a bunch of flowers arrives. It is so moving to realize that other people still remember him as being so special.

I would love the person to know how very important and special it has been. Now when the children find the flowers on the front doorstep, they just run in and say "It's 'Love and blessings' again."

Zilla Hawkins has now succeeded her husband as Churchwarden of Holy Trinity Brompton. She and her family are closely involved with many church activities.

10

"I grew dependent on alcohol at a very early age. I was drinking to make things easier and to try and forget things."

The story of Martin and Catherine Bennett

From the age of 12, Martin Bennett was the victim of a man who gave him drink, abused him, and forced him to keep everything secret. It went on for almost a decade. Here he tells the effect it had on his life and how God lifted the "terrible burden of guilt" and changed his life one afternoon in May 1993:

I was brought up Catholic, but thought that God was something that you may come across after you're dead. I wasn't too sure. As time went on, my attitude changed and I became very anti-God, anti-Jesus and anti-religion.

When I was around 12 years old, I was abused by a teacher in my school. He was a Catholic teacher, a single man and a high-profile member of the local church. It went on for a number of years.

He used to get me very drunk. The first time I remember drinking Scotch was when I was at his place and he used to do things

203

to me when I was drunk, a lot of which I can't remember. I think that's partly me blocking it out. He was an alcoholic. I can't remember many times when I'd be with him and I wasn't drinking or drunk. He put me in a position where I couldn't get out, and made me imagine that everything I did was wrong but that it was supposed to be kept secret. If I told other people about it then that would be very bad indeed. He would tell me secrets, confiding in me about other teachers and other people in the community. I was therefore forced into a situation where I was emotionally attached to him when I didn't want to be. My way around it was to switch off my emotions completely.

I left that school when I was 13 and went to secondary school so I got away from him in the school environment but in fact it got worse. As I got older, he'd take things away from me that I would need. It would start with things like my train pass. It might be money, my passport or anything like that. He'd take them away if I didn't contact him. So I would have to contact him and then the whole cycle would start up again. I was always covering my tracks—leading a double life in fact—from very early on. He was perceived to be a fine, upstanding member of the community. My parents did not know what was going on. Half the time they knew I was with him and that was acceptable to them because they still thought we had an OK relationship. No one knew what was going on, although I suspect my brothers had an inkling but were scared to broach it. I think they were frightened to think this could be happening. And I would have denied it to the ends of the earth.

I got to the point in my early twenties when I still hadn't completely broken free from it. I was still seeing him off and on, but it wasn't with the same intensity. I knew I had to try and get away. I traveled around the world for two years or so, and he used to track me down in Australia and things like that. As a result of all this—and I do connect the two very strongly—I grew very dependent on alcohol at an early age. I was drinking to make life easier and to try and forget things because I realized that if I drank enough, everything became a bit of a blur. It blocked things out of my mind. This continued for many years. I was drinking heavily from about 16 or 17. The whole business was a huge great lead weight and I assumed that I'd carry that around with me always.

After I came back from traveling, I got involved with drugs. When I was 20 I was hospitalized for long periods of time with attacks of acute pancreatitis, which can be an alcohol-related disease. When I had these attacks I was given high levels of pethidine, which is a very strong painkiller to which I became addicted. I was told not to drink but this also became part of my double life as everyone assumed I wasn't drinking and all the time I was. It was part of my life that went into the "secret file." Most of the time I would go to sleep quite drunk.

I started off drinking a small amount of Scotch or vodka every day, but ended up drinking an awful lot by the end. It was usually vodka because I had heard people say you can't smell vodka. But if you wake up the next morning still drunk it doesn't matter what you've been drinking. During my longest stay in hospital, at Middlesex, they were giving me Heminevrin to help with the alcohol withdrawal, pethidine to help with the pain . . . and I was drinking at the same time.

I had been going out with a girl named Catherine for a while and she realized something serious was going on. Eventually, it all came to a head, and thank God it did. I was 26 years old. I went to see various psychiatrists, psychologists, psychoanalysts, and psychotherapists. Some were OK; some were awful; some were useless. I was still very reluctant to let everything out, but it was obvious to everyone that I was an alcoholic, so I went to a detoxification center for about three months down in Epsom.

When I was at the detox center, the story of the schoolteacher and what he had done began to come out. I never wanted anyone to know about it. I didn't want to tell the police and I didn't want a big to do made of it. But when people said, "What if he's doing it to someone else?" then I felt morally obligated to talk to the authorities. As far as I know he was never prosecuted. But he's not teaching anymore and he can never teach again.

Then I went to a halfway house on Queenstown Road, Battersea, and that was good. I had stopped drinking and that was great. I was really making progress. Catherine stood by me throughout this time. She was my constant source of strength and support. Without her I don't know what would have happened. Our relationship was obviously an awful lot better because I had stopped drinking. But there were still a lot of things that weren't right. I had the occasional relapse with alcohol and these were very difficult times for Catherine. We were married in July 1992 and at that stage I hadn't been in the hospital for a few years. We were married in a church, as both our parents were Catholic and it just seemed the right thing to do. (I didn't really get married in church for any other reason.) At the time, I was working for a film company as a camera technician.

Then in November Catherine heard from her cousin about the Alpha course at Holy Trinity Brompton. She thought she'd go along and see what it was like and caught the last half of the current course and thought it was really great. I thought she was getting involved in some sort of cult and was a little bit concerned. However, she's a very sensible girl and so I thought that it couldn't be anything too bad. Nonetheless it was certainly nothing that I wanted to get involved in. I would argue with Catherine a lot. My inbred dislike for any religion came out and it got to the point where she wouldn't mention it to me any more because she knew I would want to argue.

Then Catherine got her cousin, Madeleine, with her husband, Con, her brother Michael, her sister Clare, her sister Anna, and Anna's boyfriend Tim, all to do the next Alpha course which started in January 1993. They'd troop off every Wednesday night, and then went off to the weekend away and came back on an incredible high. Of course it was just emotionalism to me. I was still very, very cynical about the whole thing. Catherine would go off to church on Sundays and, for a time, she would ask me if I would come to church. I always used to refuse, but then after a while I stopped to think about it. There was such a change in Catherine.

She seemed to have an inner peace. I thought, *I'm married to her. I really ought to check this out because if I don't, I won't know if I've missed anything.* So I came along to Holy Trinity Brompton on a Sunday evening and thought, *Gosh, what a bunch of fools.* But the one thing that stuck in my mind was the worship. Ric Thorpe was the worship leader then and I saw in him someone very much like myself. He just seemed a normal person. Every time he got up on the stage he looked like he was still laughing from a joke that someone had told him before he got up. I thought, *I want to know what that joke is all about. I want to know why he looks so happy. And why are all these people so happy?*

So I went along the next week on the strength of that, and Catherine prayed (I didn't know this until later on) that I'd be touched by the Holy Spirit during the service. And I was. I didn't realize what it was at the time but I just felt this incredible peace come over me. During the worship, I broke down in tears. I was sitting down and everyone else was standing up and I was crying, crying my eyes out and I couldn't figure out what was going on. I was in floods of tears. I couldn't stop it. I put it down to emotionalism and getting a bit caught up in the event. I was still quite anti-Holy Trinity Brompton but I decided I would do the Alpha course to give it a chance.

I went along to the first Alpha evening and agreed with most of the things I heard about the historical evidence of the existence of Jesus and the Bible and I thought, *Yes, that's pretty good. I don't believe it, but that's pretty good.* But then I thought, *If I'm going to get any benefit from this, I ought to discuss it with someone and try to clear away some of the confusion.* I decided to call Nicky Gumbel the next day. I said to myself, "I'm going to try calling him twice and if I don't get to speak to him then that's it. I will have tried." I called the first time and he was out and I thought, *This is looking good.* I called the second time and he was there and said, "Yes, come over and see me today at 5:30 P.M."

So it was that on a summer's evening of May 6, 1993, at 5:30 P.M., I went over to Nicky's place. We went into his backyard and he said to me, "Tell me a bit about yourself." And I told him my life story. What was strange was I told him everything right off which I'd never really done before. I'd been to see psychiatrists and psychologists and bits and pieces had come out but I just sat there in that backyard in Clapham and it all came out. It all seemed to be coming out in surprisingly frank detail, which had never really happened before and, after about half an hour, he said to me, "Well, do you feel like praying?" And I said "No, not really," because I didn't. But he said, "OK. You don't have to pray but I'm going to pray." So I said, "Fine. Go ahead." He prayed aloud for me, and as he was praying I decided, "OK. I'll close my eyes."

And this incredible peace came down on me. It was an overwhelming presence of goodness. Everything seemed so safe. He just continued praying and after a while he said, "I feel a very strong presence of God. Do you feel it?" I said, "Yes, I do as well." I couldn't believe it! And he said, "Well, look, I've got this prayer written down in *Why Jesus?* Do you think you're up to praying it now?" And I said, "Yes, I think I am." Everything was pointing in that direction for me. It was a prayer turning away from everything I knew that I'd done wrong and asking God to come into my life.

In it is the line that says, "I forgive all those who have wronged me"—or words to that effect—and Nicky said to me that he wanted me to include the name of the guy who had abused me when I was younger and to say that I forgave him. This was quite a thing for me.

The whole idea of forgiving him was totally beyond me—totally beyond my comprehension. But I said that I forgave this man. I said it three times, and each time my burden got lighter, so that by the third time I felt I was rising up into the trees. I felt an incredible release of this weight that had been dragging me down. It was lifted from me. I knew that I'd forgiven this person and that God had forgiven me. I had carried around all the guilt for such a long, long time. It was quite incredible!

I opened my eyes again and there were tears pouring down my face, and it was the same with Nicky. He said something to the effect that he never fails to be surprised and amazed by the power of God. And I said, "Well, I agree!" What had happened to me was something that was amazing—so powerful, so relevant, and so unique. There was nothing like that when I went to see any of the psychiatrists or whatever. There was no comparison. It was total cleansing. Total forgiveness is way, way beyond anything you'll ever find in a book—any sort of Jungianism, or Freudianism, or anything like that. They just pale by comparison to forgiving, being forgiven, and starting a relationship with Jesus.

We had a friend coming to supper that evening and I wanted to tell Catherine what had happened. I saw our friend trying to park outside, so I ran out the door shouting back to Catherine: "I've just been to see Nicky Gumbel and I've given my life to Christ." And she thought, *What!* But once she understood what I was saying she was delighted. It was lovely.

Incidentally, the fellow who came to dinner that night wasn't a churchgoer, but has just done the Alpha course and is helping on the current Alpha course.

I went and told my mother the next day and I've never seen her happier. It was incredible. She had been praying for me for a long time. I drove down the highway to my parents' house with tears streaming down my face listening to tapes of praise and worship music. I needed windshield wipers for my eyes really. There were lots of tears of joy, happiness ... Oh, unbelievable happiness. It was great!

My father, who is a more traditional Catholic, also recognized that something quite significant had happened to me. I wrote to my in-laws, who had also been praying, and they were very happy. The following Sunday in church Sandy Millar invited anyone who wanted to receive the Holy Spirit up to the front. I went and, as I was prayed for, I felt the Holy Spirit rushing into me. He filled me up. I had been feeling a little bit vulnerable, but once I really felt I'd gotten the Holy Spirit on board I thought, *I can cope with anything*. I had that power and that reassurance.

I continued with the Alpha course and everything began making sense to me then. All my pseudo-intellectual arguments disappeared. All the cynicism left. It was incredible! I was happy! It has made such a difference to Catherine and our relationship. We have been to a few weddings since ours and the marriage vows spring out of me now. They mean so much more. We try to pray every day and have a prayer group with the people I met on my first Alpha course. I pray for the man who abused me on occasion. I've realized that he's obviously a very lonely, very mixed-up, very sad person. He's not a problem for me anymore.

It has all been such an answer to prayer. Catherine was praying her head off during the time she was going to Alpha without me. She had a prayer diary and we've been looking back at it. It's got things like "Prayed that Martin goes to church." That's got a check by it. "Prayed that Martin does the Alpha course." That's got two checks by it. "Prayed that Martin becomes a Christian." That's got a great big check by it, and lots of other checks with a little smiley face!

Life has not been easy for Martin and Catherine Bennett since giving their lives to Jesus Christ. For much of that time they longed for a child and, on top of that, Martin came close to death after being brutally stabbed by a complete stranger. Here they tell how God has been with them through it all.

Martin:

When I became a Christian, God took an awful weight off me. But it wasn't like everything was completely wiped clean. I was, however, a completely new person, and in some respects, never looked back.

I went through quite a few changes as a Christian, slowly handing things over to God. Catherine and I began reading the Bible and praying together. That became a very important time for both of us, although it took us a little while to get used to it.

We decided that we would always try and pray before we went to sleep at night and we generally still keep to that. It is a wonderful way of wrapping up the business of the day and handing everything over to God. Now I always feel as though there is something missing if I go to sleep without praying with Catherine. We became more involved in church life. We joined a home group and found that very helpful because you could open up and pray with people at very intimate levels about whatever issues you were going through at the time.

About three years after I became a Christian, in July 1996, I went into the hospital with pancreatitis [*inflammation of the pancreas*], a condition I have suffered with since I was 20 and which occasionally flares up—causing excruciating pain, sickness, and nausea. I was in the hospital for about a week. The day after getting out of the hospital, I went to see my brother, who lived on the second floor of a block of apartments in Battersea.

I used the back entrance and, as I went through the doorway, I noticed someone leaning against the wall. It seemed a little odd. Instead of going past him, I decided to go back out and use the other entrance, but as I was doing that he quickly came up behind me.

He shouted at me, saying I owed him some money and that he wanted it. I didn't know what he was talking about. I could tell immediately that his eyes were very peculiar. He looked as if he was on drugs or something. By now he was standing about six feet away and he continued swearing and shouting at me as if he knew me.

I went to take my wallet out of my trousers and as I did that he suddenly struck out at me. It felt as though he had punched me in the stomach. I fell back against the wall and he ran off.

I was a little shaken, but not much more than that at the time. I straightened myself up. Then I looked down and saw there was a knife sticking out of my stomach, just under my ribs on the left side. I didn't think I was badly hurt because I didn't feel much—just a cold sensation. I pulled the knife out—it was a kitchen knife seven or eight inches long—and decided to go around to a clinic I knew was just around the corner.

Holding my stomach, I walked rather shakily out of the apartments. A woman was coming toward me. I will never forget her reaction when she saw me. She looked terribly frightened. I said, "I think I have been stabbed." Then my legs gave way and I collapsed toward her.

There was a man doing some work on an apartment window nearby who saw what happened and thought I was attacking her, so he ran down. Then an elderly woman came out from an apartment and brought me a pillow to put under my head. Suddenly there were police all over the place and an ambulance. I didn't pass out. It still wasn't very painful at that stage at all. It seemed okay. I think it was more the shock.

> **! I pulled the knife out—it was a kitchen knife seven or eight inches long.**

When I was in the ambulance it started getting pretty sore and by the time I got to the hospital it was very painful. When we got there, it was a bit like ER [*the television program*]. It was as if I was just a lump of meat and there were seven or eight people around me putting tubes here, there, and everywhere. I understood they needed to establish that my lungs and kidneys hadn't been damaged. Gradually all these people left as each vital organ was checked.

Finally I was just left with a surgeon and a few other people. They gave me some strong painkillers intravenously, so that helped the pain quickly. Then Catherine showed up, thank goodness. They didn't think that anything had been punctured, but they wanted to do an ultrasound to establish exactly what damage had been done, and hopefully mend it by microsurgery. While I was waiting for the ultrasound the pain got worse and worse and my blood pressure suddenly dropped. The surgeon became very worried and I was rushed into the operating room at once for an emergency operation. That was really quite frightening. It was probably more frightening for Catherine and the others, because I was really out of it.

The operation went on for several hours and, basically, it involved opening me up from top to bottom to establish what was going on. They found that an artery had been severed and I had lost a lot of blood. When I came to, I remember the nurse saying to me that it was a miracle that nothing else was damaged. They were amazed particularly because the area where I was stabbed is so full of intestines, diaphragm, kidneys, spleen . . . I remember thinking then that it was a miracle.

I knew people were praying for me and that was a great comfort and a great help. Both Sandy [*Millar*] and Nicky [*Gumbel*] visited me soon after I got out of the operating room. I found it very difficult to pray myself at the time, maybe just because my head was so full of drugs. It was difficult to hold a coherent thought for more than a couple of seconds.

When I came out of the hospital we went to Catherine's parents to recover for a week. At first I was able to walk about 30 or 40 yards, rest, then come back. However, I was surprised at how quickly the body recovers.

It took quite awhile for me to come to terms with what had happened from a Christian perspective. I was angry and initially I felt quite vengeful.

I felt that this person should be caught and punished for what he did. The anger, combined with the desire for revenge, wasn't a great help. It tended to cloud a lot of things. I found myself becoming self-piteous and self-righteous. As time went on the anger subsided a bit. I came to see this person as almost as much a victim as myself, in terms of circumstances. He was obviously very desperate and almost certainly on some sort of drugs. He was never caught, as far as I know. The police investigation tended to lose its terror quite quickly. Initially it was treated as an attempted murder, but then that quickly went down to another level.

The police were very nice. They came and talked to me and interviewed me. I think they did their best and I looked at pictures, but it

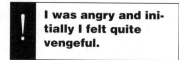

I was angry and initially I felt quite vengeful.

was so difficult because I literally saw the guy only for a matter of seconds. It is very hard to recall every feature about a face. All I could think was that he was young, white, with short hair and wild eyes.

When I returned to the area a few weeks later with Catherine, the elderly woman who gave me the pillow recognized me and told me how she and her entire church had been praying for me. She was so excited to see that I had recovered and couldn't wait to tell the members of her church. I didn't know her but I was amazed at how God works even in adversity.

I still have a thing about knives—I hate big, sharp knives left out in the kitchen and like them to be put away—but otherwise I don't really think about it a great deal. I have prayed through a lot of the issues that an event like this brings up, and dealt with them with God's help and guidance—it makes all the difference.

Catherine Bennett tells of her reaction to her husband's stabbing:

On the day of the stabbing, I got home early from work. I knew Martin was going to visit his brother that morning, so I thought I would give him a call and tell him that I was home early. I called the apartment and Martin's brother's roommate answered the phone. The first thing he said was, "Martin has been stabbed and the police are here." He added that the ambulance carrying Martin had just left for the Chelsea and Westminster Hospital. I just couldn't believe it.

My sister-in-law lives nearby so I called her and said, "Martin's been stabbed. I have got to get to the hospital. Could you come and pick me up?" At the time, one of Martin's brothers worked at the Chelsea and Westminster so I called him and said, "Martin has been stabbed and is on his way in."

When I arrived at the hospital Martin was coherent and we chatted for a while. The doctor stitched up the wound and then they said that they wanted to do an ultrasound to check that there was no internal damage. While we were waiting outside the ultrasound room, I kept looking at the nurses' and the doctor's faces. The doctor kept feeling Martin's pulse. His face suddenly dropped and he went very pale. He said, "We are not waiting here." And the next thing we were running down the hall with Martin on the bed. They rushed him up and prepped him for the operating room.

I remember Martin looking at me with an oxygen mask on his face saying, "Take this mask off. I want to give you a kiss." He later told me that he was worried whether he would see me again. It was so tense and he was being taken away from me.

I went back to the ward and sat in the cubicle where his bed had been. A very kind nurse brought me a cup of tea. I just sat there and burst into tears and thought, *I don't believe this is happening.* I knew I should pray, but I couldn't. I thought, *I just can't pray, but we have got to pray.*

So I went to the nurses' station and asked to make a phone call. I called HTB and spoke to Ali Groves [*a member of the staff*]. I said, "Ali, Martin has been stabbed. It has only just happened but I need someone to pray. He is in surgery now." I put the phone down and felt relieved that I knew that people were praying. That helped me.

He was in surgery for about three hours. During that time my sister turned up with her husband. Then Sandy Millar turned up at the hospital. He had his clerical collar on, which was quite unusual. He said, "It helps in hospitals."

The nurse came and told us that Martin was out of surgery and had gone into the recovery room. Sandy and I went up. Martin was just coming out of the anesthetic and he saw Sandy in his clerical collar and said, "Oh dear, I didn't think it was that bad!" I think he thought Sandy was there to give him the last rites.

Sandy said, "It's okay, we have just come to have a quick prayer." We prayed and then Sandy left.

Afterward, I could see that Martin felt, "Why me?" And I felt, "Why him?" There was never an answer to that. It was a very traumatic time for both of us. We would come to church and sit there, but our hearts weren't in it as they had been. I remember Sandy praying for us one time after the service. He had a picture of us in a boat in a storm. He said, "Sometimes you have to batten down the hatches and keep your head down, but keep praying and wait for the

> **!** Afterwards, I could see that Martin felt, "Why me?" And I felt, "Why him?"

storm to calm."

We started meeting on Wednesday nights with Patrick and Philly Pearson-Miles [*congregation members of HTB*]. We would talk, have a meal together and pray. To begin with it was very much Patrick and Philly doing the praying and us talking about what had happened. They helped us weather the storm emotionally, physically, and spiritually. It was terribly valuable to us.

For nearly four years, Martin and Catherine Bennett lived with the heartache of longing for a child. As time went on, they were able to tell Christian friends who prayed with them on many occasions. In July 1997, Catherine gave birth to a daughter, Lucy. Here she tells her story.

Martin and I were married in July 1992. In December 1992 we decided we would like to start a family, thinking it would just happen. For the first six months we didn't worry about it too much, but gradually I began to think, "Why isn't it happening?"

After about a year we decided to go to our General Practitioner. Psychologically, I found it very difficult to admit that things weren't taking their natural course.

He did basic tests to see if there was anything obviously wrong— which there didn't seem to be. So we were referred to the fertility clinic at St. George's. We went through various tests.

It was an arduous process. Often I would wait for an hour or so in the waiting room. I would be very strong before I went, but every time I got there I found it very difficult to cope with.

Sometimes you would see one of the specialists and then one of the doctors. I found it very upsetting. I didn't realize until every time I was in the specialist's room how difficult it was to cope with.

When Martin got stabbed and we spent the week at my parents' house, my younger sister announced that she was pregnant. Because she was younger than me, I thought, *That is not fair! Lord, why?* But, by God's grace, that was the only time I got upset when someone told me they were having a baby. God helped me so much with that.

It took me a long time to be able to tell people. I knew that my mother would tiptoe around the subject because she didn't want to meddle, although I knew that she was very concerned. It took us quite some time to be able to be so open about the whole thing. Many people prayed for us during the time that we were trying.

There were times throughout when I was up and down. Every month was a reminder that I hadn't conceived. I can remember one time feeling sheer desperation. I can remember breaking down and crying—really sobbing, thinking that this was never going to happen.

On a human level, you could only rely on the doctors. But somehow we managed to take it to a prayerful level. I knew that God could do anything, and would at some point bless us with a child. This gave us comfort and strength to carry on.

When we first started praying for a family, my brother-in-law Tim quoted from Psalm 128, which he felt was relevant for us: "Blessed are all who fear the LORD, who walk in his ways. You will eat the fruit of your labor. Blessing and prosperity will be yours. Your wife will be like a fruitful vine within your house and your sons will be like olive shoots around your table. Thus is the man blessed who fears the Lord."

We were greatly encouraged by this and often went back to it when things were difficult. After the stabbing in July 1995, we had about four months where we gave the fertility treatment a break.

Throughout the entire time various people had prayed for us. Towards the end of that time, when again I was finding it very difficult, many people prayed regularly for us. Patrick and Philly and Ric and Louie [*Thorpe—HTB staff members*] took it on themselves to pray for us to have a baby. Emmy [*Emmy Wilson, a member of the HTB pastoral staff*] and Sandy would pray with us after the Sunday services.

I remember Emmy saying to me one time, "Sometimes you feel so desperate that you can't pray about having a child. Then other people will carry you along in their faith." She really believed that we would have a child and she prayed that. I found that so encouraging.

Over the years it was the same prayer over and over again: "Oh Lord, could we have a baby?" How many times could you rephrase that particular prayer?

The whole thing was out of our hands and we came to realize that we had to trust in God. I knew that even if we conceived through treatment, it would be God. God was completely in control, however He chose to do it.

I always had a feeling in my heart that we would have a child one day. Sometimes in the middle of the day—in the middle of my work— it seemed hard to believe, but somehow when I thought about it and prayed about it, I always felt that God would give us a child.

Martin and I were able to lift each other up through times of desperation. We never seemed to go down together, which was fantastic. When I was low, Martin would be there to pray and comfort me. I remember sometimes I would be so upset and Martin would come up and give me a hug and say "Let's pray about it."

I would be thinking, *I don't want to pray about it. I just want a baby!* It was always amazing because he would feel able to pray, then I would pray too and it would make such a difference. When he was low, I would be able to pray. So God always kept one of us up if the other wasn't.

Sometimes people would ask us if we were planning to have children, not realizing that we were trying so hard. That was very difficult to cope with. I am a lot more careful now bringing up the subject of a family with other couples. I realize that you don't know what they are going through.

In September 1996, Martin and I went on the third course of a new treatment we were having. We just managed to get the last treatment in before he went off to Australia on business for three weeks.

While he was away my period was late. I thought, *I'm going to buy a pregnancy test* (assuming it would be negative). Something in me stopped from going to get one, which is what I would normally do. I thought that I would wait for Martin.

It was a Wednesday and I said, "Let's not do anything about it yet. Let's wait until Saturday."

Saturday came and I did this test—and it wasn't clear. I did another and that wasn't clear either. We read the instructions about five times. We couldn't believe that I could possibly be pregnant. We didn't stop to think about it too much. It was almost as if it hadn't happened.

The next day, a Sunday, I went off to find a druggist to buy another test. I didn't tell Martin I was doing it. I did another two tests and the last one convinced me I was pregnant. I couldn't believe it!

I went back to the fertility clinic because they like to do a scan to check that everything is okay. Before we went, I did another test because it would have been so embarrassing if I got there and I wasn't pregnant.

We went along to the hospital and they did the scan. When they had scanned me before, the screen had shown a very gray, empty area and nothing more. This time there was this tiny little blip. The doctor seemed more excited than us. She was printing out more and more pictures of the scan. She said, "There it is." She could even see the heartbeat.

We were so scared that it wasn't really going to happen that we didn't dare get excited. However, it gradually began to sink in that I was pregnant. The pregnancy itself from a medical point of view went fine, but I was very anxious. I kept worrying that I would miscarry.

I was trying to prepare myself for it all the time. I wanted to shield myself from the disappointment if the baby didn't come.

My poor mom! They were praying throughout the pregnancy for us. She was so relieved when Lucy was finally born because she knew that I was very anxious about the whole thing. When she was born I was in shock.

I just looked at her and couldn't believe that this was our baby. She was so perfect. Praise the Lord!

I don't know why we had to wait so long. I do know that it brought us closer to God. It showed us to keep on praying and to have faith. We always had that faith and to anyone else I would just say: never stop praying, never give up.

All we had left to hold onto was God. I very much feel that God is in the center of our lives and He has had His hand on us for a very long time and guided us through some very difficult times.

Martin adds . . .

We have both been through tough times. I still think we are tremendously lucky, compared to what some people have to go through. At the end of the day we have a beautiful little girl. Our faith is increased. Our faithfulness in God has increased.

We are a closer family with God in the center now. Throughout all this time, God has constantly provided for us. We are incredibly thankful for that.

Martin Bennett now works part-time in the HTB accounts department and also directs videos on a freelance basis. He, Catherine, and Lucy live in Balham, south London. "Our life is much more stable in many ways, not just financially, but prayerfully and everything," he says.

Alpha

If you are interested in finding out more about the Christian faith and would like to be put in touch with your nearest Alpha course, please contact:

Alpha North America
FDR Station, P.O. Box 5209
New York, New York 10150
Phone: (888) WHY ALPHA or (212) 378-0292
Fax: (212) 378-0262
E-mail: alphana@aol.com

This book is an *Alpha*™ resource. The *Alpha*™ course is a practical introduction to the Christian faith initiated by Holy Trinity Brompton in London, and now being run by thousands of churches throughout the UK and around the world.

For more information on *Alpha*™, including details of tapes, videos, and training manuals, contact Cook Communications Ministries, 4050 Lee Vance View, Colorado Springs, CO 80918-7100.

For *Alpha*™ orders, call toll-free: 1-800-36-ALPHA

Questions of Life

by Nicky Gumbel

What is the point of life?
What happens when we die?
Is forgiveness possible?
Who is Jesus?
What relevance does he have for our lives today?

In 15 compelling chapters Nicky Gumbel tackles the answers to these and other key questions, pointing the way to an authentic Christianity that is exciting and relevant to today's world.

"*Questions of Life* is a sympathetic, fascinating, and immensely readable introduction to Jesus Christ—still the most attractive and captivating Person that it is possible to know. Nicky Gumbel's informed approach ensures that the search for truth fully engages our minds as well as our hearts."

- From the foreword by
SANDY MILLAR

Why Jesus?

by Nicky Gumbel

Many people today are puzzled about Jesus.

Why is there so much interest in a person born nearly 2,000 years ago?
Why are so many people excited about Jesus?
Why do we need him? Why did he come? Why did he die?
Why should anyone bother to find out?

Nicky Gumbel tackles these issues in Why Jesus? a challenging, short presentation of Jesus Christ.

Nicky Gumbel practiced as a barrister and is now ordained and on the staff of Holy Trinity Brompton, London.

These publications are available from your local Christian bookstore.
Or call Cook Ministry Resources at 1-800-36-ALPHA